THE SEMINAL GOSPEL

Forty Days with Mark

George Kimmich Beach

The Seminal Gospel
Forty Days with Mark
Copyright © 2023 by George Kimmich Beach

Library of Congress Control Number: 2021904532
ISBN-13: Paperback: 978-1-64749-403-2
         ePub: 978-1-64749-404-9

All rights reserved. No part of this publication may be reproduced, distributed, or transmitted in any form or by any means, including photocopying, recording, or other electronic or mechanical methods, without the prior written permission of the publisher or author, except in the case of brief quotations embodied in critical reviews and certain other noncommercial uses permitted by copyright law.

Although every precaution has been taken to verify the accuracy of the information contained herein, the author and publisher assume no responsibility for any errors or omissions.No liability is assumed for damages that may result from the use of information contained within.

Printed in the United States of America

GoToPublish LLC
1-888-337-1724
www.gotopublish.com
info@gotopublish.com

CONTENTS

Acknowledgments v
Introduction ix
   1   The gospel 1
   2   He shall baptize you with the Holy Ghost 7
   3   And he was there in the wilderness forty days 13
   4   The time is fulfilled 21
   5   What thing is this? What new doctrine is this? 27
   6   And Jesus, moved with compassion, put forth his hand and touched him 33
   7   Who can forgive sins but God only? 37
   8   Many publicans and sinners sat also together with Jesus 43
   9   Is it lawful to do good on the Sabbath days or to do evil? . 51
  10   And he ordained twelve 55
  11   Behold my mother and my brethren! 57
  12   The mystery of the kingdom of God 63
  13   Take heed what ye hear 71
  14   What manner of man is this? 79
  15   My name is Legion 85
  16   But the woman fearing and trembling 89
  17   Is not this the carpenter, the son of Mary? 93

18	Whatsoever thou ask of me, I will give it thee	97
19	They were as sheep not having a shepherd	101
20	Evil things come from within	107
21	He maketh both the deaf to hear and the dumb to speak	111
22	Why does this generation seek after a sign?	117
23	But whom say ye that I am?	121
24	And he was transfigured before them	129
25	Lord, I believe, help thou mine unbelief	133
26	If any man desire to be first	137
27	Whosoever shall not receive the kingdom of God as a little child	141
28	One thing thou lackest	145
29	Behold, we go up to Jerusalem	149
30	Blessed is he that cometh in the name of the Lord	153
31	Who gave thee authority to do these things?	157
32	The stone which the builders rejected	163
33	And the common people heard him gladly	169
34	Take ye heed, watch and pray	179
35	Take, eat; this is my body	185
36	It is enough, the hour is come	193
37	And Peter followed him afar off	201
38	But Jesus answered nothing	207
39	And at the ninth hour Jesus cried with a loud voice	213
40	He goeth before you into Galilee	219

Footnotes 227

ACKNOWLEDGMENTS

Thanks to Barbara Kres Beach for editorial assistance for this book

Thanks to the Boston Museum of Fine Arts for licensing the cover image of "The Sower" by Jean-Francois Millet

For our grandchildren
Alec, Elizabeth, Erick, Elise, Aiden, Hadley
and their rising generation

INTRODUCTION

A pathway into the origins of the gospel is also a pathway forward from the present, toward the future we choose. This book seeks to uncover that pathway.

All that we know of Jesus and his original message is derived from a few ancient texts, among which the Gospel According to Mark is particularly fascinating and often perplexing. Mark came first among the four Gospels of the New Testament, and as such planted the seeds from which subsequent traditions, especially those in narrative form, have grown.

The Seminal Gospel is an exploration of Mark and an extended personal reflection on what his telling of the story of Jesus can mean to us today. Its two focal points are intimately related. One is Mark's text, taken so far as we are able, on its own terms. This especially means resisting the temptation to overlay our preconceived ideas about Jesus and his message on the text. The other focal point is simply what we, the readers and the author, bring to our reading. How distant our world is from the first century world of Jesus and the others vividly portrayed by Mark! And yet the humanity and passionate concerns of these people are immediately felt. In their story I recognize my own story. My hope is that readers who follow my explorations and reflections may more fully discover their own stories.

These two focal points are in tension with each other; but taken together they can generate significant insight. Like the two points which define the arcing line of an ellipse, they hold the promise of joining fuller understanding of a central religious tradition to fuller understanding of ourselves as spiritual beings. This kind of outward exploration and inward reflection will require of us a certain effort, perhaps forty days' worth—here offered in forty chapters for convenient, if not easy, daily consumption!

I

Who was Mark, and how did he come to write his Gospel? Little can be said with certainty. His use of the Greek language suggests that this was his native tongue; although literate, he was not a highly educated person. The seemingly naïve qualities of his writing make it the more appealing—for instance, the breathless expression, "and immediately!" He may have been the John Mark referred to in the Book of Acts (12: 12, 15: 37), and he may have written his Gospel in Rome as a summary of what he heard from the apostle Peter. In fact Peter is prominent in his account—sometimes in a distinctly un-flattering way! Surprisingly, all the disciples are represented as uncomprehending, querulous, and even cowardly. The conversion from a state of skepticism, self-centeredness, or simple obtuseness among Jesus' closest disciples seems to be like the experience movingly expressed by the hymn, "Amazing Grace":

I once was lost but now am found, was blind, but now I see.

Scholars think that Mark's Gospel was written near the time of the fall of Jerusalem to the Romans and the destruction of the Temple in 70 C.E., a generation after the death of Jesus. It may mark the transition from a period when the faithful relied on stories and sayings passed down by word of mouth and in written fragments, to a time when the need was felt to weave these traditions into a continuous narrative. A generation had passed and a written record became a dire need. The destruction of the Temple is remembered as one of the most calamitous events in Jewish history. This may help explain the sense of urgency and foreboding that pervades Mark's writing. He seems to be saying, "After this nothing is the same for us Jews."

Christian beginnings are understandable, then, as the effort of a small community of Jews to preserve Jewish sacred tradition by radically transforming it for a new age, putting their "new wine in new wineskins" (Mark 2: 22). This is a fundamental dynamic of human existence: *We can only preserve what is most valuable by transforming it.* Prophetic faith makes the idea of transformation explicit: "For behold, I create a new heaven and a new earth" (Isaiah 65: 17).

II

The earliest followers of Jesus were Jews who expressed their faith in the form of a story. Mark, who is known entirely from the Gospel that bears his name, was the first (from all surviving evidence) to commit the story to writing. It is called a Gospel because it carries Jesus' proclamation of *the* gospel, the good news that God's sovereign kingdom is at hand. Not only the other canonical and non-canonical Gospels but also the vast, varied, centuries-long tradition of Christianity follow the form and faith that Mark set down. Mark's Gospel stands at the head of this immense tradition. I think of the Amazon River, from the cascading torrents at its headwaters high in the Andes to its immense lower reaches, abetted by great tributaries. It becomes a vast lake moving slowly, irresistibly to the sea. No, I've never seen it in person, but Werner Herzog's film, "Aguerre: the Wrath of God" (1974), a spectacular visual parable of natural grandeur and human folly, is the next best thing.

You and I stand—or should I say, swim!—somewhere in those lower reaches of the stream of history. Trying to look back, the originating springs and early cascades are distant, belonging to a world utterly different from our own. To speak honestly about these origins we cannot ignore the separation and the strangeness this distance from us creates. And yet—speaking for myself—precisely when I see how foreign Mark's world is to my own, a moment of recognition may arise, an insight that cancels the distance between "then" and "now," between "there" and "here." These are the two focal points I referred to above. The same idea was suggested by my first New Testament teacher—later, Dean of Harvard Divinity School—Krister Stendahl. He urged his students to read a Biblical text "with two eyes," one on the text itself, seeking to understand it in its own terms, the other on our present-day understanding, letting what is unfamiliar or uncomfortable speak to us as it will. And it will, sometimes in surprising ways.

We gain insight into Mark's Gospel as we begin let go of our assumptions rooted in long familiarity. The "kingdom of God"—in Greek, *basileia tou theou*—is a pertinent example. The translation is misleading if we think of this kingdom as a place, even a "heavenly" place. The Gospel of Matthew always uses "the kingdom of heaven," probably on account of the Jewish aversion to speaking the name "God"; but this only abets the common misapprehension. Richard R. Niebuhr suggests "God-ruling" as a more adequate translation, for he notes that the *basileia* Jesus speaks of is not a physical place, nor a geographical realm; it is dynamic and unbounded, a divine presence acting powerfully in the world.[1] On whom does it act, and how? We do not immediately know; we are in a state of suspense. This *basileia* is said to be a mystery *to be revealed* in God's good time. What do we do, then, for "the time being"? We may sense, here, the mainspring of a powerfully dynamic faith, moving from expectation, to participation, to revelation. Mark leads us to speak of things we do not yet know how to speak of—a situation that is scientifically embarrassing but spiritually energizing.

In spite of various attempts to find a more adequate or contemporary rendering of *basileia tou theou*—realm of God, community of God, God-ruling—*kingdom of God* will not readily be displaced; it is too deeply rooted in our vocabulary of the gospel. Our understanding will be aided, however, if we think of this "kingdom" not in static but in dynamic terms, as something coming-into-being. James Luther Adams often accented the eventful, active character of Biblical faith; he notes its distinctive voice, "And it came to pass." As if to say: Something happened here in real time! It is important, I think, to remember that this gospel is not a free-floating doctrine or wisdom but an historical event, something that has come to pass and, for this very reason, something we live with ever after.

III

That the Gospel of Mark was written before the other Gospels in the Christian Bible is generally accepted by scholars today. Matthew's text closely parallels Mark's text, but was accorded highest authority by the early church; as a result Matthew precedes Mark in the New Testament. That Mark comes second indicates the importance accorded his testimony. Matthew has been called an "expanded edition" of Mark; it is much longer and it "corrects" Mark's text at various points. That the texts of Luke and Matthew reflect knowledge of Mark is a judgment drawn from precise comparisons of the texts.

Matthew and Luke are apparently ignorant of each other, but follow roughly the same narrative structure as Mark; therefore they independently depend on him. The absence in Mark of much other material found in Matthew and Luke—much of which they share with each other—confirms that Mark was not influenced by them. Rather, he influenced them, and they added material from other sources, and especially the source called *Quella*, or "Q" for short.[2] The differences between Matthew, Mark, and Luke should not lead us to exaggerate the disparities. The first three Gospels are called "synoptic" because they can be *seen together*, that is, read in parallel with each other. This highlights the similarities and the differences between the texts. Students of the New Testament view these differences with the help of books that set the Gospels in parallel columns.

What will you miss, reading Mark? Most notably, Matthew's "Sermon of the Mount" and Luke's so-called "Sermon on the Plain" (Matthew 5-7 and Luke 6: 20-49); also their wholly different Nativity stories (Matthew 2 and Luke 2); also, in Luke, the most famous and appealing of Jesus' parables, "The Good Samaritan" and "The Prodigal Son." It seems, then, that they read Mark (or the same sources that Mark used), but Mark, coming first, has not read them.

The Gospel of John is another matter, for John is mainly interested in providing a theological interpretation of Jesus as the Christ. By the time we reach John, usually considered the last-written of the four canonical Gospels, the "messianic secret"—already attenuated in Matthew and Luke—has disappeared from the account. This does not mean that the author of John's Gospel was ignorant of the historical or geographical facts of Jesus' life; at various points he seems to be more accurate than the other Gospels. But the discourses of Jesus found in John have the feel of finely wrought creations which embody John's theology. John, too, follows the pattern established by Mark in his final chapters, relating the final week of Jesus' life. This suggests that the Passion Narrative—told in Matthew 26-27, Mark 14-15, Luke 22-23, and John 18-20—was the earliest part of the tradition to be formed as a continuous narrative. It is interesting to note that accounts of the Resurrection appearances of Jesus, which follow the Passion Narrative, diverge most widely among the four Gospels, and are absent altogether from the earliest manuscripts of Mark. This suggests that they are symbolic witnesses of faith, not historical memories.

The non-canonical Gospels, mostly known only in fragmentary form, seem (in general) to have been written later than Mark. The most complete example is the so-called Gospel of Thomas—written in Coptic, discovered in 1945—which begins, "These are the secret words which Jesus the Living spoke and Didymus Judas Thomas wrote." Thomas is not a narrative but a series of sayings, often overlapping with sayings in the canonical Gospels, conveying Gnostic wisdom about the kingdom of God.

Two different attitudes can be taken toward the differences between the four canonical Gospels and the other ancient sources. We can say: To gloss over the disagreements among these stories of Jesus is intellectual dishonesty and to expose them demolishes faith in the Bible. Or we can say: Isn't it astonishing that the early Church kept all four Gospels as sacred scripture! This has allowed future generations, including our own, to see in their diversity not an embarrassment or a way to discredit their value, but as an enrichment that opens the possibility of fresh understandings. It liberates us from the kind of literalism that reads every story and every word as dictated from on high.

The disparity of witnesses led some Christians as early as the second century to propose combining the Gospels into a single text, but the church ultimately rejected the idea. Similarly, the proposal of some Gnostics to reject inclusion of Hebrew scripture in the Christian Bible was finally rejected. In both cases inclusiveness was chosen over a spurious "purity." In the end, I believe, the wise will choose the rich ferment of Biblical diversity, including various non-canonical sources, over a superimposed and stultifying unity.

Today we see the effort of some critics, often quondam fundamentalists, to pare down the Gospels to precisely what (they believe) Jesus said and did, eliminating everything that can be ascribed to the religious and cultural viewpoint of the authors, writing a generation or more after Jesus' death. This path tends to overlook the inherent problem of seeking out and finding a Jesus who fits the preconceptions of our time. This is not a new issue. More than a century ago it was quipped that modern scholars peer into the deep well of Biblical "higher criticism," see a reflection, and declare with astonishment, "That's Jesus!"

When we read the Gospels for what they are—texts witnessing to a passionately held faith, faith in a transcendent reality lying beyond rational definition—and respond to that witness out of our own spiritual awareness and need, then we are reading these ancient texts in quite a different way. Not everything in them will speak to us; some parts may repel us, some parts may simply baffle us, and some other parts may break through the strangeness and move us at the core of our being, as they have moved countless generations before us.

IV

I have incorporated the text of the Gospel of Mark so that the reader has each segment under discussion fresh in mind and readily available for reference. Initially I chose to use the King James Version (KJV) because it could be reproduced without the copyright restrictions. But as a result of rereading the KJV I've concluded that the reader will feel rewarded for having revisited this classic work of the English language. For the sake of clarity my commentary frequently cites the recent translation by the great classics scholar, Richmond Lattimore; see *The Four Gospels and the Revelation*, (New York: Farrar, Straus, Giroux, 1962).

There are many excellent modern translations (not to be confused with paraphrase versions) that the reader may want to refer to along the way. To my taste the KJV and Lattimore are the best of both worlds.

In a review of *The Restored New Testament*, by Willis Barnstone, (*The New York Review of Books*, July 15, 2010), Frank Kermode notes that the author "gives high praise to Richmond Lattimore's [translation of the Gospels]." Kermode comments, "What remains surprising is the continued vitality of the King James Version of 1611, . . . Having left indelible marks on secular and religious literature generally, [it] remains on the whole secure in the affection of Anglophone readers, but it is often archaic and inaccurate."

Two famous mistranslations in the King James Version are the "horns" ascribed to Moses (the original Hebrew says "rays of light" emanated from his head after his encounter with God), and the "virgin" who would give birth to the Messiah, foretold in Isaiah and identified by Christians with the Virgin Mary (in the original she is simply a "young woman"). Such outright mistakes are rare, Kermode's offhand judgment notwithstanding. The King James Version translators worked from the best Hebrew and Greek texts available to them, making comparisons to Latin and to earlier English translations, notably Matthew Tyndale's. The language of the King James Version was kept somewhat archaic by intention; if the translators felt this would lend dignity to their text, they succeeded.

V

This book culminates a labor of research and writing which has extended, desultorily, over several years. From time to time I've asked myself, to what end did I embark on this journey? At length I have answered: to rediscover the origins of the gospel, the good news, brought by Jesus. In my attempts (however desultory!) to follow the pathway he blazed for us, I have sought to understand where it leads today.

This study has taken the form of a devotional and educational exercise. Without originally so intending, I came to divide Mark into forty segments. Some readers may want to make the reading of Mark's Gospel a spiritual practice during the forty days of Lent. But any forty days or more days will do! Taking time for patient reflection is what counts.

The commentary is intended to stimulate and focus the reader's understanding of the story of Jesus that Mark tells. We do this best, I think, when we actively interrogate the text, asking, for instance:
- Who does Mark think this Jesus is, and what do I think about him?
- Setting aside all the ideas about Jesus I've picked up over the years, what puzzles me, or surprises me about Mark's way of telling the story?
- We often hear people say they are "spiritual" but not "religious." Why does Mark's Jesus not use either of these terms?
- What insights do I gain into what it means to be faithful—for Mark in his world-age? And for myself in this world-age?

In his essay, "Naming God," the noted philosopher and Biblical scholar, Paul Ricoeur, writes:

> Naming God, before being an act of which I am capable, is what the texts of my predilection do when they escape from their authors and their first audience, when they deploy their world, when they poetically manifest and thereby reveal a world we might inhabit.[3]

In this book Mark is the text of my predilection, and I find that it invites me to name God in my contemporary life-experience.

For those who are accustomed to questions of defining God, or of proving (or disproving!) God, *naming God* may seem an exceedingly odd notion. But with spiritual awakening comes the paradoxical recognition that *God is by definition indefinable.* And still more certainly, the recognition that attempts to prove or disprove the existence of God founder on their presumption of having defined God before they begin. (Often they will say, "Well, everybody knows what 'God' means! The only question is, does this God exist?" But the premise in this line of thought is entirely false.)

The present work is a personal and reflective commentary on the Gospel of Mark. More pointedly, it is an invitation to the *meta-noia*— the radical rethinking of my experience that Jesus' first words in Mark, the first Gospel, call for. Professor Ricoeur helps frame the central question of the inquiry into this *text of my predilection*. Does it *deploy* and *poetically manifest* a world we might inhabit—a world in which the gospel is available to us as a main-spring of faith? More simply stated: Does this ancient text enable me to name God in my contemporary experience?

Consider that your first answer may be, "No," or perhaps, "No, but I'm intrigued." Religious understanding requires, I believe, not just sight but insight, breaking through the crust of appearances and being grasped by something vastly deeper. So *caveat lector!* Before you enter Mark's world, consider that it may prove seductive.

ONE

The gospel

Mark 1: 1 *The beginning of the gospel of Jesus Christ, the Son of God.*

The second book in the received Greek text of the New Testament is headed *Kata Markon*, "According to Mark." Mark's first words serve as the book's title. A variant in the ancient manuscripts occurs; Richmond Lattimore's translation of this verse, cited above, omits the phrase, "the son of God," but is otherwise the same as the King James Version. Lattimore is not editing the text on his own, of course, but is following critical editions of the Greek text, in which an important family of ancient manuscripts exclude this phrase. (Scholarly texts of the Greek New Testament have footnotes indicating variant readings found among all the most ancient known texts.) Since all texts tend to be elaborated in time, not abbreviated, it seems likely that at some point the phrase, "the son of God," was added after "Christ." The Greek, *Christos*, translates the Hebrew, Messiah.

It seems likely that Mark originally headed his text simply, "The beginning of the gospel of Jesus Christ." "Christ" is a title, not a name, conferred as an affirmation of faith; for this reason I ordinarily follow the theologian Paul Tillich, who spoke of "Jesus, the Christ," or "the New Testament picture of Jesus as the Christ."[4] The meaning of this title becomes, then, a central question.

We refer to Mark's work as *a* Gospel, one of the four canonical Gospels of the New Testament. We might think that Mark is saying, "My telling of the good-news-story of Jesus Christ begins here." More likely, Mark is saying: *The gospel itself*, the good news of something wonderful happening in the world—happening even now—began in this way.

Readers may assume that "the gospel" of Jesus refers to his "teachings," comprising wisdom and ethical precepts. While the gospel includes teachings, it is something more. The text before us is not a compilation of sayings, sermons, or parables, but a narrative. Still, the story Mark tells includes many things that Jesus said, or else were attributed to him by early Christian tradition. The story comprises words that were remembered, retold, elaborated, and at various times and places written down. Like Socrates, he wrote no book. He may not have said many of the things ascribed to him, or he may not have said them in the form or context that we have. We cannot be certain in virtually any particular instance. In addition, Jesus and his first disciples spoke Aramaic; while a few Aramaic words are preserved in the text of the Gospels, all are written in the vernacular Greek of the time, called *koini*. Even Thomas, an ancient Gospel discovered in the Coptic language, is believed to have been originally written in Greek.

All this is material enough to keep a thousand scholars at work for a very long time. Here we are concerned with the Gospel of Mark. The text itself— with its ancient variants—is what we have. It is seminal not only for other works of its type but for a vast religious and cultural stream that flows from it.

Seminal does not mean entirely original. Mark not only hugely influences; he is hugely influenced. He draws upon an ancient religious and cultural heritage, Jewish and Gentile, preceding him. Jesus himself is presented as a faithful Jew, and one whose teachings are not novel. The ancient prophets, too, spoke of mercy, justice, righteousness, truth-telling, and peace. What seems distinctive about Jesus is not the content of his teachings but the immediate, intense, and radical way he asserted them. What we find in Mark, then, is something like the narrow waist of an hour-glass, the central place which gathers the past from many sources, and sends a vast and diverse future flowing outward in all directions.

This book invites us to focus on a single text, the Gospel of Mark, not on what we can know about "the historical Jesus." Some commentators have said that everything in the Gospels has been imagined, and there is no "historical Jesus" standing "behind" the text. Two considerations lend credence to this radically skeptical view. First, there are almost no independent historical records from Jewish and Roman sources, aside from a few references to his followers, attesting to the life of Jesus of Nazareth. Second, the Christian sources that we do have are not consistent with each other, and often seem to fit facts (or what are supposed to be facts) into preconceived conceptions, such as the fulfillment of scriptural prophesies. Uncovering the man who "stands behind" the text is not a simple process. He seems only to be known by his listeners, or as a consequence of his interactions with them. Patently, those effects were immense, yet who is he, himself? Or was he dreamed up?

It is virtually impossible to demonstrate from non-Christian sources that Jesus of Nazareth existed and was the sort of person portrayed in the Gospels. Nevertheless most scholars, including those who are highly critical of New Testament records about *what* can be knows about Jesus, continue to believe *that* the man and his story told in the Gospels has an historical, factual core. One reason for this obdurate belief is the sense we gain from the Gospels that the Jesus portrayed in the Gospels is not an imagined construct, but a distinctive, individual personality. The distinctiveness is brought into strong relief in the work of the distinguished scholar, Guenther Bornkamm:

> Every one of the scenes described in the Gospels reveals Jesus' astounding sovereignty in dealing with situations according to the kind of people he encounters. This is apparent in the numerous teaching and conflict passages, in which he sees through his opponents, disarms their objections, answers their questions, or forces them to answer them for themselves... . The same can be seen when he encounters those who seek help: miraculous powers proceed from him, the sick flock around him, their relatives and friends seek his help.... Again and again his behavior and method are in

sharp contrast to what people expect of him and what, from their own point of view, they hope for.5

Bornkamm goes on to cite more instances of Jesus' character, displayed in his actions and interactions, and says, "The Gospels call this patent immediacy of Jesus' sovereign power his 'authority.'" I call it his creative freedom.

All religions give prominence to stories of beginnings and endings, the whence and the whither of our existence. We can even say that this dual concern is central to religion itself. The Bible begins with *Genesis* and ends with *Revelation*, the book also known as *Apocalypse*—a word that has taken on fantastic connotations, but at its root simply means "uncovered." Much of our religious language is freighted with long-accumulated religious and superstitious ideas; it is helpful, then, to go back to original usages and to ordinary, "secular" language. Even with words we may think we know perfectly well, such as "mystery" and "apocalypse," the dictionary's clues to etymology can be enlightening. When Jesus spoke of "last things" he meant things now veiled in mystery which are ultimately to be "uncovered," to be seen and known. To speak of them begins the process of uncovering, for it creates an expectation of light breaking through the darkness of our present existence. Properly speaking, "apocalypse" is not an expectation of disaster, but of revelation.

Beginnings and endings are prominent in the story Mark sets out to tell.

Early in the 20th century Albert Schweitzer published his famous study, *The Quest for the Historical Jesus*, concluding with his own view that Jesus' entire teaching turned on a "thoroughgoing eschatology," a total orientation toward "last things," or the end of the world. The book shocked liberal Christians. It did not reflect the Jesus they thought they knew, the Jesus of the Golden Rule—to do unto others as you would have others do unto you—and the Great Commandment—to love God and to love your neighbor as yourself. Liberal Christians have always liked this "religion of Jesus" and often set it in opposition to the orthodox "religion about Jesus." How strange and upsetting, then, that a great liberal Christian like Albert Schweitzer should point out that this neat opposition is not clear-cut, and that the radical ethic of Jesus, in which self-giving love and forgiveness are so prominent, is rooted in a "thoroughgoing eschatology": everything Jesus said and did was premised on his vision of an end-time.

Schweitzer felt that the Jesus revealed in the Gospels is a stranger to the modernist view he had himself shared. He concluded his monumental book:

> He comes to us as One unknown, without a name, as of old, by the lakeside, He came to those men who knew Him not. He speaks to us the same word: 'Follow thou me!' and set us to the tasks which He has to fulfill for our time.

Those who do so, he says, "shall learn in their own experience Who He is."[6]

Soon thereafter Schweitzer undertook preparations to become a medical missionary in Africa. His "quest for the historical Jesus" led him to transform his brilliant career as a Biblical scholar, an organist, and a musicologist into a life of personal renunciation and humanitarian service. Curiously, though, Schweitzer did not abolish eschatology, but transformed it from something cosmic and mythic into something personal and historical. His existential decision responded to the age in which he lived, an age he experienced as losing its moral and spiritual center. An eschatology of cosmic transformation became an eschatology of personal transformation, a life lived for others.

Schweitzer wrote his famous book, which chronicles the century-and-a-half long search for Jesus' historical identity, as a summing up. The book itself was eschatological insofar as it marked the end of an epoch, a Europe drifting into what Raymond Aron called "the century of total war." In the African rain-forest, suddenly coming upon a herd of bathing hippos, he tells us, the universal and affirmative moral principle that he had long been seeking suddenly came to him: "*Reverence for life.*" An ending had become the point of departure for a new beginning.

The world in which the Gospel of Mark appeared was in many ways similar to the epoch that began in Schweitzer's time and continues in our own time, a century later. Ours is a world of immense creative energy—and yet, a world of destructive and deadly conflict; a world of profound intellectual achievement—and yet, a world of intractable cynicism; a world of protracted and deadly struggles for justice—and for this very reason, a world seeking to recover its moral and spiritual center. My first mentor in ministry, Joseph Barth, of King's Chapel, Boston, gave a sermon I have not forgotten on a line from an ancient Jewish exile: "How shall we sing the Lord's song in a strange land?" (Psalm 137: 4) How, then, in our own Babylonian captivity? Here begins the gospel.

TWO
He shall baptize you with the Holy Ghost

Mark 1: 2-8 As it is written in the prophets, Behold, I send my messenger before thy face, which shall prepare thy way before thee, the voice of one crying in the wilderness, Prepare ye the way of the Lord, make his paths straight. John did baptize in the wilderness, and preach the baptism of repentance for the remission of sins. And there went out unto him all the land of Judea, and they of Jerusalem, and were all baptized of him in the river of Jordan, confessing their sins. And John was clothed with camel's hair, and with a girdle of a skin about his loins; and he did eat locusts and wild honey; And preached, saying, There cometh one mightier than I after me, the latchet of whose shoes I am not worthy to stoop down and unloose. I indeed have baptized you with water: but he shall baptize you with the Holy Ghost.

The story is set deep in the history of the Jewish people, echoing Isaiah's prophecy of a messenger who would come "before your face." This being the rough and ready John the Baptist, we could say "in your face!" We can also read the words as a contemporary demand, for reading the prophets seriously means reading them as addressing our own age. *We* are those before whose face the messenger comes.

We often think that prophets "foresee," but Isaiah "fore-hears." He hears "the voice of one crying in the wilderness," words Mark cites from Isaiah 40: 3. "Wilderness" means a wild, uncultivated place, a desert—not as we think of wilderness, a trackless forest. Save for the coastal plains, desert encroaches everywhere in Palestine, a land so arid that you wonder how anyone could call it "a land flowing with milk and honey."

This is the story, then, of one who fulfills ancient prophecy of the coming of Messiah, *the anointed one*, smeared with oil as kings have been throughout history as a mark of divinely chosen royalty. This story is rooted in the sacred tradition of the Jews, and draws its significance from its prophetic as distinct from its priestly interpretation. The heart of prophetic interpretation calls for the transformation of tribal loyalties into a universal loyalty. It celebrates not worldly triumph and power—James Luther Adams called it "the vaunted spirit of the age"—but the coming of a new world-age, an "age of the Spirit" (see Joel 2: 28ff. and Acts 2: 14ff.). It is a transformation that happens through commitment and suffering, often with the humiliations of a smear campaign. During the height of McCarthyism in America, in the 1950s, Joel Henry Cadbury—New Testament scholar and Quaker—suggested that *Messiah* be translated, *the smeared one*.

The messenger is John the Baptist, who lives in the wilderness—"he ate locusts and wild honey"; he opens a pathway for one greater than himself, one who "is coming after me." Scholars see evidence of an independent movement led by John, probably one to which Jesus was drawn. Mark reflects the way in which the early Christian movement supersedes John the Baptist's movement by incorporating him, albeit in a supporting role.

As in the Book of Exodus, the wilderness in which "the children of Israel" wandered for forty years is a place of spiritual purity and receptivity, a place of complete dependence on divine grace. It is during this period that Moses receives the Decalogue, the founding charter of Judaism (see Exodus 20). Similarly, the wilderness is where Jesus will be baptized, as the Israelites were "baptized" by their crossing the River Jordan into "the promised land"—that is, the land promised to father Abraham (Genesis 12: 1), the land of the Canaanites.

Mark says "all the people of Jerusalem" came out to be baptized by John "in the river Jordan, confessing their sins." "All the people" sounds impossibly hyperbolic. Maybe Mark just gets carried away by his story. "Confessing their sins" sounds formulaic; what is meant is an act of conversion, or re-commitment, putting on a new self in place of the old. To picture the scene is to put ourselves into it: casting off crooked thoughts and devious deeds by passing through waters that drown whatever is old and weighs us down. Symbolically, these waters wash away the human stain, so that we may rise again to be warmed by the life-giving sunlight. Baptism signifies the gift of rebirth, the new beginning we will need many times in a lifetime. Mark's terse prose invites imaginative participation, painting in the sketchy picture with vivid colors, for this is a scene fraught with emotional background.

Portentous symbolism is contained in John's word, "I baptized you with water, but he will baptize you with the Holy Spirit" (Lattimore translation). Jewish tradition speaks of the divine Spirit (*Rauch*), the presence and felt power of God, but not as a divine Person distinct from the Creator. How did Christian doctrine come to think of three distinct-yet-mingled divine Persons—Father, Son, and Holy Spirit? What does it mean to call the Holy Spirit (or Holy Ghost, the old English term) the Third Person of the Holy Trinity? Michael Servetus, the Spanish physician and anti-Trinitarian theologian of the 16th century: "I say that the Holy Spirit is God's Spirit acting in the human being." For his denial of the Spirit as a distinct member of a Holy Trinity and other heresies he was tried and burned at the stake in Calvinist Geneva. Apparently John Calvin feared that the Protestant revolt against the Catholic Church had opened a theological Pandora's Box of new ideas; faced with a brash and brainy Michael Servetus, they wanted to proclaim their Trinitarian orthodoxy. They did so with a vengeance.

During the time of the English civil war, a century later, it was said of the brash, confident Calvinists, "There is nothing so dangerous as a Presbyterian just off his knees." Ironically, Unitarianism throughout its history has emerged on ground ploughed by Calvinism—Transylvania and New England are cases in point. Broadly speaking, this seems a consequence of Calvin's way of pressing the Augustinian doctrine of predestination to its breaking-point. But the knife cuts both ways; my colleague Richard Boeke recalls church historian Roland Bainton saying, "Scratch a Unitarian and you'll find a Calvinist."[7]

An old painting of St. Augustine shows him on a beach with a small boy who holds a large spoon; it illustrates his comment that explaining the Holy Trinity is like trying to empty the ocean with a spoon. The best explanation of "the mystery of the Holy Trinity" I have heard—this may not be entirely orthodox, if only because mysteries of the faith cannot, by definition, be demystified—came from Richard R. Niebuhr in a theology class at Harvard Divinity School. He spoke about the early 19th century split between the liberal and orthodox Congregationalists of New England over the doctrine of the Trinity; the liberals were finally "outed" as Unitarians, and only later embraced the label. The resulting schism might have been averted, he said, except for a misplaced literalism regarding the Trinity on both sides. He noted that the three members of the Trinity were originally called Persons not in the sense of distinct divine beings but as roles or personas of the one God. Judaism spoke of the divine Spirit but this was understood as the "breath," the life-giving or inspiring action of the one God. In the Greco-Roman cultural context *persona* had a distinct meaning; ancient Greek dramas were originally sacred enactments, with masks worn by the actors to represent archetypal *personae*. No Hindu would be surprised by the idea that the divine should present to us various faces or *personae*.

Thereafter the Christian God was said to have three *personae*, or perhaps four, if we count the Virgin Mary. In the fourth century the Trinitarian terms Father, Son, and Holy Spirit became orthodox. I think of them as Creator, Mediator, and Spirit, functional terms that express aspects of God in relation to us; the divine "in itself" remains hidden from our understanding. The Trinity names three masks of God, both hiding and revealing identity, as all masks do.[8]

"Spirit" is associated with life; Adam came alive when God breathed the breath of life into a clay humanoid figure (Genesis 2). Spirit is also associated with the sparks that ignite fire—both fire itself and the warmth and danger of fire. Fire destroys; it also purifies and renews. Natural processes of transformation evoke awareness of similar moral and spiritual processes. John the Baptist was a famously fiery preacher of Judgment Day; he was also witness to the descent of the dove, the sign of divine peace and favor, at Jesus' baptism.

In this passage Mark is calling up images from sacred history of the Jews, as well—Noah's flood and Elijah's fire. Elijah, the archetypal prophet of ancient Israel, uses prophetic utterance to ignite the fire on Mt. Carmel in his life-and-death struggle with the priests of Baal (1 Kings 18: 37-38). Elijah did not die, in spite of the threats of king Ahab, but was taken up to heaven in a chariot of fire; he is expected to return as a precursor to Messiah. In this heaven-sent *persona* the early Christians cast John the Baptist. The sacred drama continues.

Appreciating these symbolic references enlarges our understanding of Mark; his story is replete with ancient and archetypal meanings. To read the story as literal is not only to miss much but also to misread it. A non-literal reading is also necessary if we are to ask: What does this mean to *me*? Do I live with expectation and hope? Do those whom I love do so as well?

The gospel is about expectation and hope, and the transformation that carries us from here to there. To live and to be awake to our living is to live toward the future. To live toward the future, with faith, is to live with hope-filled expectations. To live in the face of death, without denial, makes this kind of awakening and this kind of expectation difficult. "For the Time Being," W. H. Auden's Nativity drama, offers a concise definition of faith—*existential* in that it requires a decision:

> To choose what is difficult, all ones days,
> As if it were easy, that is faith. Joseph, praise.[9]

Prosaically, it is difficult to live with a life-affirming hope and without the denial of death—knowing that living toward the future is finally living toward death. It calls for an inward turn. May it call forth a spiritual transformation.

THREE

And he was there in the wilderness forty days

Mark 1: 9-13 *And it came to pass in those days that Jesus came from Nazareth of Galilee, and was baptized of John in the Jordan. And straightway coming up out of the water, he saw the heavens opened, and the Spirit like a dove descending upon him: And there came a voice from heaven, saying, Thou art my beloved Son, in whom I am well pleased. And immediately the Spirit driveth him into the wilderness. And he was there in the wilderness forty days, tempted of Satan; and was with the wild beasts; and the angels ministered unto him.*

Many things happen in one short paragraph—putting it mildly. The story is anchored in historical facts: Jesus came from Nazareth of Galilee, and there at the river Jordan was baptized by John. This would seem to reflect a definite memory that Jesus became a follower of John the Baptist, and his ministry begins with this event. We may imagine that John already knew Jesus and had marked him for "great things." But the text gives no hint of this—indeed, Jesus' baptism is not said to be different from anyone else's. Except, of course, for the word that came to him from above! The story is at once both ordinary and extraordinary. In this as in many instances, the Gospel of Mark sets the precedent for the way that succeeding generations envision the gospel.

In Mark's telling, we see that Jesus' mission involves submersing himself in the life of his age and his people, sharing in their longing for a new life and a new Israel. His withdrawal into the wilderness does not signify a spirituality of withdrawal from the world but a preparation for entering more fully into it. In order to be part of the people of our times and their struggles, we too must be capable of standing apart. Mark does not pause from his breathless telling, but we will, if we read deliberately and reflectively, if we read this as a story we are in.

Mark moves on quickly to Jesus' so-called temptation in the wilderness—"*And immediately the Spirit drove him out . . . .*" How curious, "drove him out," as if it were something he resisted and had to be driven to do. Surprises like this may serve as flags: *this calls my unstated assumption into question.* We may have assumed that Jesus naturally or easily did whatever he did, but this sentence suggests that the vocation to which he consents has not been deliberately chosen; it is a challenge thrust upon him that he must either meet or fail. He is more human than we thought, for this is a dynamic of human existence that any of us may have felt at significant moments in our own lives.

The Spirit first descends upon him, and blesses him; the Spirit then drives him and tests him. In the world Mark evokes Jesus will often find himself constantly beset by the spirit world, both divine and demonic.

How else does one become a prophet, a mahatma, or a saint, than by being put to the test? So the trial begins "immediately"—a word that is characteristic of Mark's way of letting one event tumble after another. He is not trying to be dramatic. Nowhere does he strive for literary effect. He speaks unselfconsciously of events as seeming to happen under divine compulsion. There is no time to pause and ponder the course of events; history is a moving train. The world-age itself is under pressure and the people who populate it are set off-center, displaced, and driven. Mark may be he author of his Gospel, but he sees God as the author of the gospel he has to tell.

The parable of "the good Samaritan" is a lesson in taking mercy, concluding with Jesus' directive, "Go and do likewise" (Luke 10:33). What directives might we take from the story of Jesus' "temptation in the wilderness"? To give it a try:

I would likewise not hold myself aloof from the storms of our times, nor from any human community caught up in them. I would let myself be driven out into our wilderness world. I would likewise consent to being baptized into the spirit and hope of my age. I would likewise choose freely, but in a way that signified something beyond this particular choice in this present moment.

I would live by this benediction that I wrote long ago and have pronounced many times:

> *Thou, Life of all our lives,*
> *let us be joined each unto each as one community.*
> *May we know now the calling of our time,*
> *and the grace that is offered us this day. Amen.*

Reading further in Mark we hear "a voice from above," addressed to Jesus: "You are my son whom I love," or in other translations, "You are my beloved son." The King James Version capitalizes *Son*, perhaps because it is a Trinitarian title. Scholarly commentaries on this passage discuss a question that seems not to have crossed Mark's mind: Who heard these words—Jesus only, or Jesus and John, or Jesus, John, and everybody else gathered at the riverside? The question is natural, especially if we ask, how could Mark know about the voice? The question arises, I think, from a misplaced literalism; nobody literally heard a voice from heaven. The voice from heaven spoke these words (or something like them) because the sacred tradition that carried these words makes eminent sense of the person of Jesus: He was chosen as one worthy of this life, this ministry, this gospel. He did not seek it out; he consented to it.

Great interest focuses on the precise meaning of "the voice from above" because the words bear on the developing Christology—the conception of the meaning and identity of Jesus as the Christ—in the early Christian church. Here a couple of Biblical comparisons are instructive. First, Psalm 2: 7, which apparently Mark (or his received tradition) is quoting: "I will tell you the decree of the LORD: He said to me, 'You are my son, today I have begotten you.'" The notes in the Oxford Annotated Revised Standard Version (RSV) tell us that these words are "a formula of adoption whereby the king became God's son," and provide further Biblical references reflecting this concept.

Second, compare the parallel passage, Luke 3: 22, which ends: "a voice came from heaven, 'Thou art my beloved Son; with thee I am well pleased.'" Luke's words are identical with Mark's. However, a footnote on a variant reading found in some ancient manuscripts of Luke comments, "Other ancient authorities read 'today I have begotten thee,'" the same language as Psalm 2: 7.

The entire question of how Luke's words came to differ in various ancient manuscripts, and which manuscript came first, is discussed in fascinating, scholarly detail by William Malone.[10] I'll offer my own conclusion: Psalm 2: 7 became the basis for the Christian claim that Jesus, being of the lineage of king David (by tradition the author of the Psalms), was declared by God to be *Messiah*, that is, the anointed ruler. It also implies an "adoptionist" Christology, that is, the idea that Jesus became the Christ (Messiah) by divine adoption *at the time of his baptism* by John. This belief was reflected in the Christian creeds; the Nicene Creed, dating from the 4th century CE, preserves the original language of adoption but adds a further clause to assert that the adoption, or "begetting," preceded the creation itself: " . . . one Lord Jesus Christ, the only-begotten Son of God, Begotten of his Father before all the ages… ."[11] The added phrase, "before all the ages," alters the meaning of "begetting" from *adoption* to *incarnation*: Jesus did not *become* the Christ, but *was* the Christ eternally. The creed asserts what became orthodox belief in the fourth century, namely, that Christ is co-eternal with the Father and the Holy Spirit, and that He "became man."

Mark's Gospel contains no Virgin Birth nor *any* birth narrative because his Christology, adoptionism, doesn't need to go back to his birth. The Nativity and Virgin Birth stories in Matthew and Luke developed later than Mark and independently of each other. Their accounts differ from each other and are entirely absent from the Gospels of Mark and John. Apparently Mark believed that Jesus' ministry—to bring God's healing presence and rule to this world—began with his baptism by John the Baptist. Perhaps the alternative reading of "the voice from heaven," found in some manuscripts of Luke, *was also Mark's original language*, following the language of Psalm 2. "This day I have begotten thee" may have been altered in early copies of Mark precisely to *remove* the idea of adoption.

Why are these minutia interesting? I had always thought that "only-begotten Son" was an assertion of Christ's *unique* divinity and that it told *how* "God became man" in the Incarnation. Indeed, old-master paintings of the Annunciation, showing the Holy Spirit as a dove shooting impregnating rays toward a kneeling Virgin Mary, beautifully illustrated the "begetting." But Biblical history suggests an earlier meaning, in which "begetting" is metaphor for adoption. For the Romans of this era, to have no son and heir (death in battle took many young men) was tragic; but the tradition developed that a man could "beget" a son by choosing a child not his natural son. He would publicly declare words not unlike "thou art my beloved son." In the ancient world adoption was a common practice among rulers and land-owners, for whom having legitimate heirs was essential to the maintenance of dynastic wealth and power.

Whether the words of "the voice from above" signify divine favor, or the simple act of choosing his representative-on-earth, this voice could only be the voice of God. Jesus is not just sent on a mission; in fact, no particular mission is prescribed. It's as if God were saying, "You will know what to do." St. Augustine famously said, "Love, and what you will, that do"—an astonishingly liberal principle of ethics, but hardly lax: the admonition is frontloaded with a very difficult imperative: live for love's sake alone.

James Luther Adams, drawing on Augustine's thought, sees a close connection between will and love: We choose what we are drawn to, what we love. In this way freedom of will, if it is truly good will, is the partner of love.[12] My own meditation and a prayer follows:

> There is a time to be drawn into the world of work and family and public life, and a time to be with oneself alone. The more we have of the world about us, the more we shall need of ourselves and of eternity.

The world of unceasing activity, for all its brilliance, blinds us. The noise of the world, for all its pathos, for all its bravado, deafens us. Then do we seek again the quiet recesses of the soul, the dim and refreshing places of rest.

God of all power, be close to us as the pulse-beat of our own hearts. With thee we begin to move. God of all compassion, be close about us. For strength in our solitude we pray. For love's sake alone, let our lives be given. Amen.13

The Spirit "immediately drives him" into temptation by Satan. Here *temptation* means *test*, as Lattimore has it. That Satan tests the virtue and piety of a reputedly virtuous and pious man is the premise of the Book of Job: Is he pious and virtuous only because he is prosperous and healthy? The answer in Job is an emphatic *no*! Job is pious and virtuous not for the sake of reward but because it is his character. So he passes the test and at the end of the book is miraculously restored to health and wealth. Job does the right deed for the right reason.

Unlike Matthew and Luke, Mark does not say *how* Jesus was tested, leaving us to imagine some kind of soul-struggle. The simplicity of his account is powerful, I think, precisely because it does not elaborate, as Matthew and Luke do. It invites us to feel what this young man was feeling, as we may ourselves may have felt in the face of a great challenge or decision. Nevertheless, the tradition knew it was too good a story *not* to elaborate; just so, Matthew and Luke report highly imaginative tests. Refusing, for example, to turn a stone into bread, Jesus says, "Not by bread alone shall man live, but by every word that issues through the mouth of God" (Matthew 4. 4, in Lattimore's elegant and precise translation.) The saying (a parable), now well-worn with repetition, illustrates the way in which this Gospel is seminal; it generates new traditions.

Mark himself knows only that Jesus was in the wilderness for forty days (like the Israelites' forty years' wandering in the wilderness, before they could enter into the Promised Land). Yet the wilderness is closer to God than any humanly cultivated place; it is God's garden, a peaceable kingdom where the wild animals are Jesus' friendly companions and the angels, serving his need to be fed, "minister to him."

Just so, faith is an invitation to live by trust, depending upon life-sustaining resources present in the world about us. It is a peaceable "letting go." Faith is also an invitation to pure receptivity, responding to the sheer wonder of being, a gracious "letting be." Further, faith is a radically social principle, for it reminds us that we are utterly dependent upon each other. So charitable giving, cooperative endeavor, and even voting are essential works of faith. To cop another famous phrase from Matthew, in the wilderness I am "poor in spirit," which is to say, utterly *un*-self-reliant, the opposite of being "full of myself." To be poor in spirit is to be humble, not arrogant or puffed up. We are taught to be as poor in spirit as the unleavened bread that nourished the children of Israel at the outset of their wilderness wanderings.

FOUR
The time is fulfilled

Mark 1: 14-20 *Now after that John was put in prison, Jesus came into Galilee, preaching the gospel of the kingdom of God, And saying, The time is fulfilled, and the kingdom of God is at hand: repent ye, and believe the gospel. Now as he walked by the sea of Galilee, he saw Simon and Andrew his brother casting a net into the sea: for they were fishers. And Jesus said unto them, Come ye after me, and I will make you to become fishers of men. And straightway they forsook their nets, and followed him. And when he had gone a little further thence, he saw James the son of Zebedee and John his brother, who also were in the ship mending their nets. And straightway he called them: and they left their father Zebedee in the ship with the hired servants, and went after him.*

Commentators have said that Jesus' first reported words, "The time is fulfilled and the kingdom of God is near; repent and believe in the gospel," encapsulate his entire message. The Greek word for "time" here translates *kairos*, meaning propitious time, as distinct from *chronos*, meaning chronological time. His message, then, is timely in the same sense that a harvest is timely, a time of ripeness and fulfillment. Mark supplies the historical context of Jesus' message: "after John was betrayed" (Lattimore) or "arrested" (RSV). *Kairos* may also signify a time of crisis and decision, "an existential moment."

The event was notorious enough for Mark to assume that his readers know John's fate: he was murdered by the tetrarch, Herod Antipas, the son of king Herod the Great. ("Great" signifies builder on a vast scale, but hardly "great" on anyone's moral scale. After he murdered one of his own sons, Caesar Augustus himself quipped, "Better to be Herod's pig than his son.")

Jesus' call to repentance echoes John's call, except in this respect: Rather than turning from sins so that they may be remitted, Jesus calls for a turning toward the kingdom of God. Here as elsewhere in the Gospels, Jesus' message is remembered not as threatening but as promising. Still, a promise and a threat are two sides of one coin: the contrast between John's and Jesus' messages is easily over-drawn.

The kingdom of God that Jesus announces is "near"—somewhere between *not yet* and *already upon you*, or in a word, *urgent*. It seems likely that Jesus had been among the many followers of John the Baptist, and that John's arrest was a catalytic event that propelled Jesus and those who followed him to set out on their own. Mark and his circle may have wanted to show that Jesus superseded John: he was the Elijah to their Messiah. These ideas lend the sense that an ordinary, un-miraculous history underlies the Gospel accounts, but they are inherently speculative and therefore the stuff of much scholarly interpretation and debate.

Clear-sightedness is more than an intellectual virtue. It is a spiritual necessity. We commonly hear the view that Jesus expected the imminent arrival of a cataclysmic event, which he called the kingdom of God. Obviously, he was "mistaken." If Jesus' entire ministry was predicated on a mistake, we should drop the inquiry right here. A failed prediction on such a grand scale suggests a delusional pseudo-prophet. But in the realm of religious understanding the mistake is to assume that we know exactly what we are looking for before we set out to find it. Nowhere does Jesus describe the kingdom of God; he only speaks in parables, that is, in oblique metaphors that conceal as much as they reveal.

When, where, and what is this kingdom of God? It is always "near," as Lattimore has it, or "at hand," as in the King James Version. Therefore it is always "available," as Joel Henry Cadbury said; I think he meant to say that it is there for the taking—except you must actively reach out and *take it*. If so, being in existential relationship to this kingdom is intrinsic to its visibility, even its reality. Objective facts are external; they are observable and definable. Existential realities are internal; we live within them and therefore cannot observe them objectively. The great Jewish religious thinker, Martin Buber, taught us to recognize that spiritual realities are not found in *I-it* relations but in *I-thou* relations, that is, realities that are not known through objective observation but through personal participation.

The kingdom of God of which Jesus speaks is neither wholly present nor utterly future, but paradoxically both. It is a way of living *in* the present *toward* the future. Perhaps all powerful historical movements are something like that—having an electric effect upon those who wholly give themselves to them. This is a story not about some spiritual realm set apart from all ordinary, historical realms of life. It is a story about the creative spirit in human experience. Apocalypse, the idea of a cataclysmic end of the world, is not to be confused with eschatology, a consciousness of living in the present toward the future—a consciousness that transforms our sense of the present and its promise. This sense of things suffuses the Gospel of Mark. If God-ruling is consciously at hand—if I am grasped by it—then I can reach out and grasp it.

When my wife and I lived in the tangled streets laid out by cows in the colonial, pre-automobile era of Marblehead, Massachusetts, a peninsula surrounded by water on three sides, drivers would stop to ask for directions to Salem, the town next door. We would say, "You can't get there from here." First we'd enjoy their consternation, and then we'd try to explain how to back-track from where we were and find the way. To say the kingdom of God is available is to say, the good news is, you *can* get there from here.

The calling of disciples—Simon and Andrew, James and John—is Jesus' first act. Neither the lonely prophet nor the closeted mystic, from the outset he is also a community organizer. (Those tempted to belittle the role of a community organizer should learn about Ella Bhatt, founder of SEWA, the Self-Employed Women's Association, with more than a million members in India and neighboring countries.[14])

The early Christian church is an example of a voluntary association—in fact, one of the most successful in history. Of course, its huge success eventually undermined its voluntary character, as hierarchy and bureaucratic control set in.

But just how voluntary was it, even at the outset, when all Jesus had to do was say the word, "Come, follow me," and get immediate action: "At once they left their nets and followed him." We would say he was a charismatic leader, the kind of leader who understands that free will means nothing until it becomes voluntary consent to do what in some sense "has to be done." This is what Paul Tillich meant when he spoke of grasping that which grasps us. A charismatic leader knows that doing what has to be done is a matter of discerning the tides of the spirit, the *Zeitgeist*. It is not that Jesus can command the disciples, as if he had divine authority. It is that he has *charisma* in abundance, the word we translate as "grace."

The first recorded use of the Greek word, *charis*, from which "charisma" is derived—a state of being specially gifted—occurs in Homer's *Odyssey*, when Odysseus comes to shore after shipwreck, naked, begrimed with salt and seaweed. Throwing himself on the mercy of the princess, Nausicaa, who is playing ball with her handmaids on the shore, he washes and anoints his body: "so Athene gilded with grace his head and shoulders, and he went a little aside and sat by himself on the seashore, radiant in grace and good looks; and the girl admired him" (*Odyssey* VI, ll. 235f., Richmond Lattimore translation). By his baptism in the River Jordan, Jesus too had passed through waters of rebirth and, being specially gifted by God, had become irresistibly attractive.

James Luther Adams speaks of God as "the community-forming power." He also notes that the early Christian movement became one of the most successful voluntary associations in history. Jesus' charisma did not just draw people to himself; it drew them into a dynamic new community. Who does not want to be part of something great and good? Something powerful, and therefore empowering?

A cautionary word is also in order. We must also ask: Is this dynamic new group really good? Our time is so full of dehumanizing movements claiming to be good that we must look twice before signing up for the next self-proclaimed "great and good" cause. Many have been burned by their own early enthusiasms and many by their life-long careers and causes. Probably you, and certainly I, have stumbled, and then heard and heeded the song so smoothly crooned by Diana Krall,

Pick yourself up, dust yourself off, and start all over again.

Even "after the fall" we want to be part of something great and good—knowing that nothing else will liberate our energies, nothing less will give us to ourselves.

FIVE

What thing is this? What new doctrine is this?

Mark 1: 21-28 *And they went into Capernaum; and straightway on the Sabbath day he entered into the synagogue, and taught. And they were astonished at his doctrine: for he taught them as one that had authority, and not as the scribes. And there was in their synagogue a man with an unclean spirit; and he cried out, saying, Let us alone; what have we to do with you, thou Jesus of Nazareth? Art thou come to destroy us? I know thee who thou art, the Holy One of God. And Jesus rebuked him, saying, Hold thy peace, and come out of him. And when the unclean spirit had torn him, and cried with a loud voice, he came out of him. And they were all amazed, insomuch that they questioned among themselves, saying, What thing is this? what new doctrine is this? For with authority commandeth he even the unclean spirits, and they do obey him. And immediately his fame spread abroad throughout all the region round about Galilee.*

Jesus does three things, he teaches, he heals, and he organizes. This is his ministry, his service. The content of his teaching is not, it seems, new doctrines or special wisdom but the gospel itself, the immediate in-breaking of the kingdom of God—remembering that this "kingdom" is not a place but an event. As noted above, it is an awareness of "God-ruling," an awkward term but one that conveys the sense of immediacy and dynamism. It is something that radiates power, as Jesus' charisma does.

A symbol, Paul Tillich said, is something that points beyond itself and yet participates in its being. (Tillich speaks of "being" as the fundamental ontological reality; "the power of being" is its capacity to stand against nothingness.) I understand "God-ruling" as a symbol pointing to sacred reality, the depth dimension present in all reality. I have called it "the presence of transcendence." The phrase is paradoxical, for "transcendence" is not apparent, visible, or tangible. Authority means being an author, one who speaks independently and originally. Jesus' teaching "with authority" is contrasted with the teaching of "the scribes," the religious teachers who interpret ancient sacred texts and draw their authority from their reputation as learned interpreters. No wonder they are hostile to this "upstart" who dismisses their authority and refuses to justify his own.

Jesus' "authority" is dramatized in his freedom, acting without regard to the rules and restrictions of tradition. But he does not claim to speak on his own authority; he speaks on the authority he believes God has given him. As we see in the directives he gives his disciples, a similar authority may belong to anyone who speaks within the charmed circle of God-ruling. Mark marshals evidence of this authority directly following, in stories of his healings and exorcisms. They demonstrate that the kingdom of God really is already "at hand," available to those who grasp it.

What does it mean to be a minister of the gospel? James Luther Adams recalled Dean Dan Fenn at Harvard Divinity School saying, "Gentlemen, let me remind you that Jesus was not a parson."[15] That is, he was not ministering under the authority of an ecclesiastical body, as a member of the ordained priesthood. Today the Dean would have said, "ladies and gentlemen," of course, but Adams's point was to accent what he called "radical laicism," the recognition that ministry is a function of membership in a religious community. Ministry does *not* presuppose ordination—what in British tradition is called "holy orders."

Ministry means, still today, being called to teach, to heal, and to organize. More formally these are called the *prophetic*, the *priestly*, and the *governing* offices of ministry, but these are not necessarily professional roles. Martin Luther spoke of the priesthood of all believers, and to this "radical laicism" James Luther Adams added "the prophethood of all believers." Adams also spoke of "the organization of power and the power of organization" as central to the making and the maintenance of a free faith.[16] The "governing" and "organizing" roles of ministry will be surprising and perhaps controversial only to those who have not observed what effective ministers do, leading their people to fulfill "the ministry of the laity."

Among Jesus' first followers there was no organizational hierarchy, as we see in stories of the disciples jostling over who will be counted first among them. Jesus says: Who would be a master must first be a servant. The principle is salutary when applied to secular institutions, most strikingly Robert Greenleaf's development of "servant leadership" in the realm of business management. To minister means, simply, to serve. Jesus provides the model of these three functions of ministry, which belong not only to ordained clergy but also to all persons who enter into the realm of God- ruling.

Jesus' authority resides in his spiritual power more than the supposed wisdom or originality of his teachings. The people exclaim, "By his authority he gives orders even to the unclean spirits, and they obey him." These convulsive, unholy powers come from the spiritual realm, the realm of demonic and angelic powers. They recognize him, Mark suggests, because he comes from and is in close communication with their unearthly realm, both divine and demonic. How different are these people from people today? Not very, I think. We presumptively sophisticated moderns easily exaggerate the difference.

Is Jesus an Emersonian, biding us to cast off external authorities and listen to the oracle within? No, and Yes. No, he points not so much to an *inward* as to an *encompassing* spiritual reality, something that sweeps up all people and all events before it. This is a difficult notion for us due, I think, to our tendency to sharply distinguish between internal feelings and external perceptions. But yes, there is a certain ecstatic immediacy about this mystery, this hidden-yet-revealed presence of God, and an almost Emersonian way of saying: *Seen with new eyes, all things are made new!*

The instant notoriety that Jesus gains is striking: "The rumor of him spread into the whole region about Galilee." Needy people seek him out, scribes (religious teachers) take offense, crowds gather wherever he goes, disciples—men, women, their children—follow him about. What do they want? Some want to put him to the test (although as we know he has already been tested by the Spirit). Some look for someone willing to answer "the establishment" without being intimidated. Many seek healing for themselves and their loved ones. On the simplest level, they want a sign that God notices them: they are *not* invisible, insignificant, unworthy—contrary to what the powerful and the worldly have told them.

This may be to project our own spiritual concern and longing onto people, glimpsed within Mark's text, whose cultural context is radically different from ours. But are the people themselves really so different from us? I think not. People everywhere and always name their children so that they shall not be anonymous. Doing so, they ask the world to recognize them as distinctive and valuable individuals. They believe (or perhaps they need to believe) that, where the world fails to do so, God does recognize them. Where else do we get our idea of "the dignity and worth of every human being," a value-commitment that is important to assert precisely because the world so often violates it—where else than from this transcendental faith?

Many philosophers, professed believers in God, have tried to intellectually construct a God concept. Such concepts usually present an impersonal God. God as "being itself," to use Tillich's formula, is a good example. Such philosophical designations have a conceptual dignity and satisfy an intellectual need for clarity. But passages of the Gospel like this one remind us why we still want, or want in addition, a God to whom we can address a prayer; we want to be personally recognized, known, loved, and we want to find our humanity anchored in a reality that sustains human personality. Such reflections lead us to ask about the basic motives of religious assent. Simply stated, why do we believe in God? To me it a matter of choosing a humanly habitable world and a way of walking humbly upon it.

Religious teachers do not demonstrate their case by logic or evidence. They can only say: I have taken this path; follow me as far as you will, and from there, set out on your own. I think Jesus' invitation was like that, and those who have truly followed him have found not bondage but liberation.

SIX

And Jesus, moved with compassion, put forth his hand and touched him

Mark 1: 29-45 *And forthwith, when they were come out of the synagogue, they entered into the house of Simon and Andrew, with James and John. But Simon's wife's mother lay sick of a fever, and anon they tell him of her. And he came and took her by the hand, and lifted her up; and immediately the fever left her, and she ministered unto them. And at even, when the sun did set, they brought unto him all that were diseased, and them that were possessed with devils. And all the city was gathered together at the door. And he healed many that were sick of divers diseases, and cast out many devils, and suffered not the devils to speak, because they knew him.*

And in the morning, rising up a great while before day, he went out, and departed into a solitary place, and there prayed. And Simon and they that were with him followed after him. And when they had found him, they said unto him, All men seek for thee. And he said unto them, Let us go into the next towns, that I may preach there also; for therefore came I forth. And he preached in their synagogues throughout all Galilee, and cast out devils. And there came a leper to him, beseeching him, and kneeling down to him, and saying unto him, If thou wilt, thou canst make me clean. And Jesus, moved with compassion, put forth his hand, and touched him, and saith unto him, I will: be thou clean. And as soon as he had spoken, immediately the leprosy departed from him, and he was cleansed. And he straitly charged him, and forthwith sent him away; and saith unto him, See thou say nothing to any man: but go thy way, shew thyself to the priest, and offer for thy cleansing those things which Moses commanded, for a testimony unto them. But he went out, and began to publish it much, and to blaze abroad the matter, insomuch that Jesus could no more openly enter into the city, but was without in desert places: and they came to him from every quarter.

Healings and exorcisms ("casting out devils," *i. e.*, demons) predominate in Mark's picture of the beginnings of Jesus' ministry. We see crowds of people clamoring for his curative powers. He must escape to "a lonely place" in order to pray. He must get out of town, and on to the next, "so that I may preach there also," as his mission requires. He tries to hush up the people and even the demons about these wonders, but to no avail. He also instructs a man to go to the priest who is due "the gift for your purification." Mark never represents Jesus as less than pious, a Jew obedient to the Law of Moses. The reason he so instructs the man is not, it seems, for him to stay out of trouble with the religious authorities, but rather "as a proof to them," to authenticate his being cured of leprosy. The predominant impression: Jesus has created an immense stir among the common people and they seek him out, wanting some piece of his "powerful stuff," whatever it may be. Apparently Jesus wants to hide the source of his miraculous powers; but why? Scholars call it "the messianic secret." The secrecy is to little avail; it's like lugging home a wet sack of potatoes, while a hole gapes ever larger.

Harvard professor Arthur Darby Nock provided us a classic and memorable definition: "Religion is what people *in community* do, say, and think, *in that order*, with respect to those things, *real or imagined*, over which they have no control." He was quite clear: religion is communal before it is individual and it is behavioral before it is intellectual. More simply and no less profoundly, Nock spoke of religion as "the human refusal to accept helplessness." How will you act upon that great refusal? Paradoxically, then, religion is a way of gaining a kind of control in the face of conditions utterly beyond our control. No wonder religion features miracles. Miracles are "wonders," things "too good to be true"; paradoxically, we believe in them for this very reason. They are "signals of transcendence" in an otherwise inhumane world.

Faith-healing remains as important today as it always has been among believers. Being science-minded we look askance at the phenomenon. We are wary of deceptions that feed on human desperation and fear. We think: better to solve the problem by rational and scientific means. But when scientific medicine has run its course, we may find ourselves "incurably religious" precisely in Professor Nock's sense: we refuse to accept helplessness. We may do no more than invite the presence of another person who watches over us and comforts us. Someone who ministers to our human need helps us to wrest meaning from pain and loss.

Some people—they may say they were raised in "the school of hard knocks," or claim they "have never been sick," or otherwise admit to no vulnerabilities—have difficulty accepting such gifts. They need to hear: sometimes it is better to receive than to give. As a minister I always knew that, when someone was in ill-health, you had to be there. I also often felt that I was more healed—to use the word that is hard for us—by a visit than they were. Only at hospital bedsides did I learn the art of extemporaneous prayer: "Would you like me to pray with you?" Many, I think, were not "the praying sort." I cannot remember a refusal. Willingly received, it would not be my prayer, but their own. My dictum: Begin with thanksgiving (no matter how hard it seems in the face of this person's suffering).

I also learned that it's good to have a default button in your kit-bag when the spontaneity fails you—something that's *not* in Mark, the Lord's Prayer. What's in your kit-bag?

I wonder about Jesus' having to find "a lonely place" to pray. In an Alban Institute workshop for ministers led by Roy Oswald, I learned the useful concepts, *intra-dependency* and *extra-dependency*. Intra-dependent is what you have to be when you have to depend on your own resources to lead, direct, inspire, and motivate, and of course looking good all the while. It's exhausting, and you really need some extra-dependent time—time to depend on somebody else, lie back and be taken care of, or be entertained. Oswald held up a cartoon of a man leaning forward in the front pew in church, an eager expression on his face; the caption read, "Inspire me!" His message to us ministers was that leading worship for others, a highly intra-dependent activity, was not to be confused with worshipping, a deeply extra-dependent activity.

Think of all the people crowding Jesus, wanting "a piece" of him, wanting his healing or assurance or just to be near him! Even Jesus needed some extra-dependent time. We know the feeling and the need for retreat and respite after a time of stress. It's not an escape. Robert Frost likened his life, and perhaps ours, as well, to taking down a tree the old-fashioned way, with an ax. With each swing of the ax, as with each day's labor, as with nature itself, he sees "no defeat"—"Or for myself in my retreat / For yet another blow."[17] Authentic worship, or any form of spiritual self-care, is not an escape from the world but an interlude prior to re-engaging with it.

SEVEN

Who can forgive sins but God only?

Mark 2: 1-12 *And again he entered into Capernaum, after some days; and it was noised that he was in the house. And straightway many were gathered together, insomuch that there was no room to receive them, no, not so much as about the door; and he preached the word unto them. And they come unto him, bringing one sick of the palsy, which was borne of four. And when they could not come nigh unto him for the press, they uncovered the roof where he was; and when they had borne it up, they let down the bed wherein the sick of the palsy lay. When Jesus saw their faith, he said unto the sick of the palsy, Son, thy sins be forgiven thee.*

But there were certain of the scribes sitting there and reasoning in their hearts, Why doth this man thus speak blasphemies? Who can forgive sins but God only? And immediately when Jesus perceived in his spirit that they so reasoned within themselves, he said unto them, Why reason ye these things in your hearts? Whether is it easier to say to the sick of the palsy, Thy sins be forgiven thee; or to say, Arise, and take up thy bed, and walk? But that ye may know that the Son of man hath power on earth to forgive sins, (he saith to the sick of the palsy,) I say unto thee, Arise and take up thy bed, and go thy way into thine house. And immediately he arose, took up the bed, and went forth before them all; insomuch that they were all amazed, and glorified God, saying, We never saw it on this fashion.

It's a curious scene. Four men carry a paralytic man on a pallet aloft, open a hole in the roof, and lower him through the hole—all to get their friend past the crowd and before Jesus, so that he might heal him! Rembrandt captures this crowded scene in one of his finely rendered etchings. "Jesus seeing their faith said to the paralytic, 'My child, your sins are forgiven'" The story emphasizes that faith is a necessary precondition of healing. Although his presence seems to have a catalytic effect, Jesus is not a magician.

Faith in what? At least this, the presence of the kingdom of God, the availability of its power to those who reach out for it and grasp it, and even cut a hole in to roof to get at it!

Another curious feature of this case is that the faith in question belongs to the pallet-bearers, not the paralytic himself. It is *their* faith, hope, and love, bearing him up, that does it. The healing is communally effected. So religion is, further, a refusal to accept the helplessness of any within the community of those we know and care about. How hard it would be, if not impossible, left to our own devices! Vital churches understand this and offer channels for mutual support and help.

The paralytic and his helpers remain anonymous. Surprisingly, the story then turns to the first of many instances of conflict between Jesus and the religious authorities, especially the scribes, men who are learned in Jewish law. Observing the scene and hearing Jesus' words, they think, blasphemy! Only God can forgive sins! Those who read Mark through the lens of fully developed orthodox Christian doctrine may say: "Of course, what they don't recognize is that Jesus *is* God." This explanation may come to mind, but it doesn't seem to occur to Mark. What interests him, rather, is that Jesus takes the occasion to up the ante by saying, in effect, that forgiving sins is easy compared to what now happens at his bidding: "I tell you, rise, take up your bed, and go to your house." It is an unforgettable sentence—about what?— the empowerment of the forgiven, those who live within the power and realm of God. Again, Jesus' command has a catalytic effect on others.

I like Lattimore's colloquial rendering of what the crowd said: "We have never seen the like."

We notice that sickness (paralysis, in this case) and sin are not distinguished in Mark's world. This conflation troubles us, but reflects a world in which people live among all sorts of benign and malignant powers. While this passage seems at first to be a healing story, it turns out to be a controversy story. At question once again is Jesus' "authority," the rights by which he speaks and acts. And the crux of these words and deeds is something central to the entire gospel—forgiveness. Or more precisely—the rightful capacity to forgive.

There will be opportunities along the way to reflect on Jesus' conflicts with the religious authorities, conflicts that grow ever sharper. We note that here, for the first time, Jesus refers to "the son of man" as one who has "the authority to forgive sins upon earth." He does not directly identify himself as the bearer of this title, but implies that as one who comes in this heaven-sent role, he holds this authority. The indirectness may reflect Mark's idea of the messianic secret, even though the title "Messiah," which is often sometimes linked to the title "Son of man," does not appear at this point.

Scholars have debated at length about the origin and the meaning of the title, "the Son of man"; in earlier, apocalyptic literature the Son of man is said to appear at the turning of the ages, to lead the way from the old to the new. In the apocalyptic book of Daniel we read:

> I saw in the night a vision, and behold, with the clouds of heaven there came one like a son of man, and he came to the Ancient of Days and was presented before him. And to him was given dominion and glory and kingdom that all peoples, nations, and languages should serve him; his dominion is an everlasting dominion, which shall not pass away, and his kingdom one that shall not be destroyed. (Dan. 7: 13-14)

Some suggest that "son of man" may only be Jesus' way of referring to a typical man, "everyman." But this seems odd. More likely, whatever Jesus said of himself, Mark understands this as a reference to the Messiah. Mark believes that the ministry that God has chosen Jesus to carry forward is a supremely redemptive role, and that *the community Jesus calls together is called to continue this ministry, this redemptive role, in the world*. These are formative Christian ideas still today. Mark is seminal.

What do we say? Can you or I forgive sins? To forgive is to release from guilty judgment and consequent penalty. "Forgive us our debts" makes the precise meaning of this much-used word clear: to forgive is to cancel repayment of an obligation rightly owed, or to release from punishment for a penalty rightly deserved. Can we do that on our own authority? The question is more complex when the law or the security of the community is at stake in the decision. Crimes may be committed against individuals, but in a nation of law they are considered violations of the nation. Then only the head of the legal community can pardon a violator of the law. Morally, however, individuals or families who are the victims of crimes can act personally, for their own reasons, to forgive. Sometimes they do this even after the state has rendered its legal verdict. This moral action is, I believe, more important for healing human relationships than legal pardon.

The fact remains that there is something radical and shocking in Jesus' attitude and action; he pronounces a man's sins forgiven without even knowing what those sins may be. Leo Tolstoy, in his novel, *Resurrection*, raises one of the most radical questions that we can ask: "By what right does one person punish another person?" It goes to the root of our humanity: Are we in truth the same as other people or not? Our resistance to saying, yes, is palpable. But if not, what fate of incurable conflict do we seal? Forgiveness is rooted in self-understanding as much as, perhaps more than, understanding others. When we can say, "There but for the grace of God go I," we are ready to forgive. This is another seed from the seminal gospel.

It is easy to lose our way amid these complexities. Most cases of wrongs being done between people do not reach the level of legal crimes, and these wrongs tear the fabric of interpersonal life. Forgiveness is abetted by the contrition of the other, but contrition is not a necessary condition of forgiveness. Sometimes forgiveness freely given becomes, in itself, occasion for the offender to feel and express contrition. In such a case the act of forgiveness is more like divine grace, an undeserved gift, and may effect a spiritual transformation. Is this the kind of forgiveness that Jesus announces?

Forgiveness is not a magical potion. Some people refuse to admit that they have done anything wrong: They cling to their refusal past all reasonable bounds, while others refuse to offer forgiveness past all reasonable bounds. This is the stuff that human tragedy is made of. And it is all the more tragic, all the more difficult to undo, when whole groups are involved in victimizing deeds. Recent history offers a horrifying list of examples of mass criminality, and occasional struggles to overcome its effects through such devices as commissions for "truth and reconciliation."

What is a sin? The etymology of the underlying Greek word, *hamartia*, suggests that to sin is "to miss the mark," that is, to miss or fall short of the standard of righteousness. If sin is so commonplace, not to say inevitable, then obviously we must be about the business of forgiving again and again, even "seventy times seven," or we would be totally paralyzed and unable to get anything done. Is it the scribes' thought—which Jesus "reads" without their having uttered it out loud—that since sins are wrongs committed against God, only God can forgive sins? Perhaps. But that distinction seems to have broken down in this brave new world of the gospel. Here God's holiness is no longer a realm apart, but wholly present, wholly resident in our relations with one another. So too with Jesus' "Great Commandment": Loving ones neighbor as much as, or even more than, you love yourself. This is the moral and spiritual equivalent of loving God with all your heart, soul, and mind (see Mark12:8-31).

EIGHT

Many publicans and sinners sat also together with Jesus

Mark 2: 13-28 *And he went forth again by the sea side; and all the multitude resorted unto him, and he taught them. And as he passed by, he saw Levi the son of Alphaeus sitting at the receipt of custom, and said unto him, Follow me. And he arose and followed him. And it came to pass, that, as Jesus sat at meat in his house, many publicans and sinners sat also together with Jesus and his disciples: for there were many, and they followed him. And when the scribes and Pharisees saw him eat with publicans and sinners, they said unto his disciples, How is it that he eateth and drinketh with publicans and sinners? When Jesus heard it, he saith unto them, They that are whole have no need of the physician, but they that are sick: I came not to call the righteous, but sinners to repentance. And the disciples of John and of the Pharisees used to fast: and they come and say unto him, Why do the disciples of John and of the Pharisees fast, but thy disciples fast not? And Jesus said unto them, Can the children of the bridechamber fast, while the bridegroom is with them? As long as they have the bridegroom with them, they cannot fast. But the days will come, when the bridegroom shall be taken away from them, and then shall they fast in those days.*

No man also seweth a piece of new cloth on an old garment: else the new piece that filled it up taketh away from the old, and the rent is made worse. And no man putteth new wine into old bottles: else the new wine doth burst the bottles, and the wine is spilled, and the bottles will be marred: but new wine must be put into new bottles.

And it came to pass that he went through the corn fields on the Sabbath day; and his disciples began, as they went, to pluck the ears of corn. And the Pharisees said unto him, Behold, why do they on the Sabbath day [do] that which is not lawful? And he said unto them, Have ye never read that David did, when he had need, and was an hungred, he, and they that were with him?

How he went into the house of God in the days of Abiathar the high priest, and did eat the shew bread, which is not lawful to eat but for the priests, and gave also to them which were with him? And he said unto them, The Sabbath was made for man, and not man for the Sabbath: Therefore the Son of man is Lord also of the Sabbath.

Here follow three more controversies with the religious authorities: First, eating and drinking "with sinners and tax collectors," that is, the impious and those who work for the Roman oppressors. Second, the question of not fasting, unlike the rigorous Pharisees and the ascetic disciples of John the Baptist. Third, the question of harvesting on the Sabbath, work that seems contrary to the Jewish law.

In each case, as with the question about the right to forgive sins, Jesus gives a sharp answer, a memorable rebuke. The first challenge comes from "the scribes and the Pharisees," which sounds formulaic but refers, respectively, to those learned in the Mosaic Law and to the party of strict keepers of the Law. The second refers to both the disciples of John the Baptist (a historical indicator that John had his own loyal following) and to the Pharisees. The third refers to the Pharisees alone.

Sometimes it seems that friends come and go while enemies accumulate. For Jesus, both accumulated rapidly—which is a major theme of the story Mark tells.

Notable, here, is Mark's consciousness of a sharp division between John's followers and Jesus': John's are ascetic and judgmental; Jesus' are celebrative and accepting. This may be more formulaic than historical. John stands in the old age and announces a new; Jesus brings the new age. In the division between them we see the Christian conviction that the coming of Jesus marks an epochal shift, to a *novus ordo seclorum* (new order of the ages), the motto on the back of U. S. dollar bills. This motto is the most striking thing about the coming of the "good news" which is the gospel.

"The strong do not need a physician, but those who are in poor health." This theme builds upon the theme of moral transformation: "I come not to summon the just, but the sinners." Respectable people down through the ages must always have gagged over these words; they undercut easy moral judgments. How did the Puritans ever get past these passages? Abandoning all self-righteousness seems to be a precondition of the coming of the kingdom of God. I call it the principle of humility, the willingness to say, "This is what I think, *but I may be mistaken.*"

On the question of fasting, the image of a wedding party is lifted up, and the simile of the bridegroom at the feast, as if to say, "That's the way it is with us today." An ominous note is also sounded: one day it will not be so happy with us, for "the bridegroom" will be taken away. The idea of the Church as "the bride of Christ" seems planted in these metaphorical seeds, waiting to be fully developed.

Then comes a parable about using "new cloth" to patch an old coat. Here Lattimore translates more precisely: Jesus speaks of an "unfulled" patch, that is, woolen cloth that has not been thickened and shrunk by a process of moistening, heating, and pressing. (Ah, the things you learn when you look up obscure old words!) Another parable with the same message follows, about the foolishness of putting new wine in old wineskins. (I do not picture Jesus reeling off parables in rapid succession; I picture Mark gathering similar sayings of Jesus into one context.) Notably, these parables appeal not to learned or scriptural sources but to common experience. Their import is not some esoteric idea or wisdom but immediate consciousness: a new age is upon us, and now everything is changed!

Unlike the previous, more typical parables, Jesus now appeals to Jewish tradition, taking the example of King David. Like kings everywhere, it would seem, David took license to skirt inconvenient provisions of the Law (an anachronistic sin, in any event, since Jewish Law had not been codified fully at the time of David). Mark records no genealogy of Jesus, as Matthew and Luke do; they want to establish that he is a "son [descendant] of David" (see Matthew 1: 1ff. and Luke 3: 23ff.). This tradition may have developed after Mark's Gospel was written; in any event, Jesus never seems to have claimed Davidic descent for himself. Still, the accusation that he put himself "above the law" fits the idea of him as Son of David or Messiah or King, or even Community Organizer! Other community organizers have been charged with putting themselves above the law: recall Martin Luther King, Jr.'s defense of his actions in "From the Birmingham Jail," responding to the charge that he fomented violence while preaching nonviolent resistance.

Fasting and long faces belong to the old age; Jesus belongs to the new age, and brings feasting and joy. His word that the Sabbath was made for us, not we for the Sabbath, reflects the same radical revaluation. The statement is also another parable, that is, a particular case which illuminates a general principle: Laws and tradition are, in the last analysis, subordinate to human needs and good purposes. This is an example of what moral philosophers call teleology, an ethics that typically asks, what good ends are being aimed at by this action? The contrasting view is called deontology, an ethics which typically asks, what moral rules or laws apply to this action? Eschatological theology tends to favor teleological ethics; it is less concerned about observing traditional rules, values, or pieties than about the ends for which these practices (such as Sabbath observance) were originally instituted. The responsible person is not one who is careful never to break the rules, but one who takes responsibility for the consequences of her or his actions.

Jesus' radical stance does not, of course, settle the issue. For instance, a utopian scheme like Communism broke down traditional moral rules, but notoriously failed to take responsibility for the consequences its actions. Lenin scoffed at the notion that "the ends don't justify the means." Dismissing this moral scruple, he said, "If the ends don't justify the means, what does?" The moral problem he conveniently overlooked, of course, was the assumption that he knew with absolute certainty what the good ends of society are; thus any action, however brutal, that would achieve them was justified. These ethical discussions, never definitively concluded, are likewise seeded by Mark's Gospel.

Mark himself only knows that "the Son of man"—might I call him "the child of humanity"?—is the ruler of the Sabbath and not ruled by it. The folk song, "Lord of the Dance," sung to the familiar tune, "Simple Gifts," springs from and carries forward this sacred and celebrative spirit. The Sabbath is made for joy, for dance, for moving with the Spirit.

The same spirit sparks renewed moral sensibility. "If our virtues did not go forth of us / 'Twere all alike as if we had them not." (Shakespeare, *Measure for Measure*). Wear your virtues lightly, without pride, not like heavy cloaks, however beautifully embroidered. "Nothing astonishes men so much as common sense and plain dealing" (Emerson).

Albert Schweitzer's recognition, more than a century ago, that Jesus' thought and action are rooted in a "thoroughgoing eschatology" was previously noted (Chapter One). In the ensuing years scholars debated whether Jesus held a concept of eschatology as "future" or as "realized," that is, already present. Some scholars conflate eschatology, that is, ideas or doctrines concerned with "last things," with apocalyptic visions of catastrophic endings—the sort of mindless melodrama that is the stock in trade of contemporary film entertainment. Failing to distinguish the two, commentators either see Jesus as a deluded apocalyptic visionary, or else they separate Jesus' message from eschatology altogether, arguing that he was a wisdom teacher something like the Cynics of ancient Greece. However, both the "apocalyptic" view and the "wisdom teacher" view of Jesus cancel Mark's vision of Jesus as a prophet of radical transformation.[18]

My reading of Mark proposes that Jesus does not distinguish between a "future" and a "realized" eschatology; he affirms both a kingdom of God that is future—thus an unshakable ground for hope—and a kingdom of God that is already present—thus potentially available to those who grasp it in the present. Eschatology is one of those big, academic-sounding words that is unlikely to find its way into everyday conversation. Religious communities need to find new, expressive language to capture the sense of being "purpose driven"; for instance, theologian Marianne Micks has coined the phrase, "the future present," to express a fresh vision of communal worship as "a summoning of the future and a shaping of the present."[19]

Jesus never wrote a book. He never, so far as we know, propounded a theory of last things, an eschatology. But his words and deeds constantly reflect an eschatological consciousness: an intense awareness of the pressure that the future exerts on the present, transforming our sense of the present as a time of awakening and decision. In eschatological consciousness "our hopes and fears" become palpable in expectation, apprehension, intention, decision—all the modes of consciousness that orient ones life to the future rather than to the past, and ones deeds to their consequences rather than correctness.

This is neither a conservative nor a liberal vision, as we use these terms today. Religious liberals, who typically shy away from any idea of eschatology, probably find the assertion of liberal theologian James Luther Adams surprising: "Liberalism requires eschatological orientation." Adams believed that liberalism in religion or politics is not primarily a rationalist or intellectualist outlook, but an outlook that "takes time seriously" and is therefore open to fresh insights and new commitments in response to "the tides of history." Jesus says "now is the appointed hour," and calls us to our appointed task. Our tasks, like the cultural furniture of our lives, are entirely contemporary. Yet here is an ancient text that "reveals a world we might inhabit," as Paul Ricouer said. From this angle of vision, the passages of time and distance make no difference.

In Mark's Gospel a growing urgency attends the conflicts with religious authorities, the pressure of the crowd, and the convulsive outcries of demons. The story is impelled toward a climax already well-known to Mark's readers. "The sense of an ending" (Frank Kermode) pervades the telling. It is not just Jesus' message that is eschatological; it is the story he tells by the course of life that he chooses and somehow, at the same time, is chosen for him. This is the human condition in which we too share: our freedom and our destiny converge at an endpoint beyond our understanding.

Do we sense that this Gospel tells of a real person, however strange this ancient, vanished, and often fantastic world may be? If we say, "no, the whole thing was made up," our attitude toward the story changes. But Mark's progeny, believers and skeptics alike, have shared the sense of an underlying historical reality. They could not have said, as relativistic modernism does, "It's *only* a story and we all make up our own versions." The story Mark is telling is one that a man told with his very life; in other words, the text has the quality of a report by witnesses, told and retold and no doubt embellished. The fact that it is loaded with loose ends and anomalies only increases our sense that no one has made all this up. It is also a story filled with religious meaning, and as such is an intensely personal report. In what sense, then, is this a true story? The truth of the story lies in its being read as a sacred parable, and a story we are in, a story that brings the truth of ourselves to light.

NINE

Is it lawful to do good on the Sabbath days or to do evil?

Mark 3: 1-13 *And he entered again into the synagogue; and there was a man there which had a withered hand. And they watched him, whether he would heal him on the Sabbath day; that they might accuse him. And he saith unto the man which had the withered hand, Stand forth. And he saith unto them, Is it lawful to do good on the Sabbath days, or to do evil? To save life, or to kill? But they held their peace. And when he had looked round about on them with anger, being grieved for the hardness of their hearts, he saith unto the man, Stretch forth thy hand. And he stretched it out: and his hand was restored whole as the other. And the Pharisees went forth, and straightway took counsel with the Herodians against him, how they might destroy him. But Jesus withdrew himself with his disciples to the sea: and a great multitude from Galilee followed him, and from Judea, and from Jerusalem, and from Idumaea, and from beyond the Jordan; and they about Tyre and Sidon, a great multitude, when they had heard what great things he did, came unto him. And he spake to his disciples, that a small ship should wait on him because of the multitude, lest they should throng him. For he had healed many; insomuch as many had plagues. And unclean spirits, when they saw him, fell down before him, and cried, saying, Thou art the Son of God. And he straitly charged them that they should not make* *him known. And he goeth up into a mountain, and calleth unto him whom he would: and they came unto him.*

Here follows another, more spectacular healing (a man with a "withered arm"), another challenge from his enemies, and another rebuke to his challengers, this time in the form of a question they will be unable to answer: Is it permitted to do good or evil on the Sabbath? Note that the question asks not just "is it permitted to do good," but "to do good or evil"; this implies that *not to do good* in such an instance of human need is itself *to do evil*. The question puts those who challenge him in a moral bind. Since it cannot be lawful to do evil on the Sabbath or on any other day, then how can it be unlawful to do good—ironically—even on the Sabbath?

In these disputes Jesus seeded the anti-legalism of the early Christian church, exemplified by Paul's theology of justification by faith and renewed by subsequent reformist movements among the churches. Even the most liberal churches generate elaborate rules to regulate the interactions of clergy and parishioners, past and present; we are left asking absurd questions, such as, is it lawful for a minister to befriend a parishioner?

The Pharisees do not question the healing itself but its timing, for it is said to violate the Sabbath. But the gospel is all about changing our way of thinking, about *metanoia*, being turned around. Here is the first mention of another party, the Herodians, that is, supporters of king Herod and subsequently, his son Herod Antipas. They are said to conspire with Pharisees against Jesus. The curious fact that Mark shows more interest in the controversy than in the man who is healed probably reflects not indifference on Jesus' part, but rather Mark's central interest: a new understanding for faith. Similarly, Jesus also shows more interest in the crowds, surging around him, than in the good *mana*, the healing power, that he dispenses. Again, it's "the unclean spirits"—denizens of the spirit world—who recognize him, and again he tries to shut them up. He keeps his true identity veiled in mystery, according to Mark—leaving us to wonder, why? These "unclean spirits" are not obliterated, but they are temporarily defeated when they acknowledge Jesus' superior power and authority: "When they saw him they fell down before him and cried out, saying, You are the son of God." How strange—the demons see what the disciples themselves cannot!

Orthodox Christians naturally hear the demons' outcry, "You are the son of God," as affirming Jesus as the second person of the Trinity—Father, Son, and Holy Spirit—adopted at the Council of Nicea in 325 CE. But Mark's concept, apparently, is that Jesus was adopted—metaphorically "begotten" as noted in the discussion of Jesus' baptism—as God's son.

A few words on the nature of evil are in order; there's no shying away from it, although the tender-hearted often shrink from the very word. Demonic evil—the twisting of what is in itself good to evil ends—is a persistent phenomenon. You cannot eliminate it from human existence, but you may be able to bring it back in line, face it down, or repress it with an authentic and powerful good will. The gospel of Jesus dramatizes this struggle.

To speak of "the demonic" is to admit a *relative* dualism—a dualism that is temporal, not eternal. This is not the same as the idea of "the satanic," which implies an *absolute* dualism; the story of Satan as God's eternal foe, inexplicably and implacably evil, is a myth; that is, it is a story of supernatural beings. In reality there is no "satanic" evil, *pure* evil, for no such thing can exist in the natural order, a conviction that follows from the Biblical idea of creation (Genesis 1). Just so, I learned at my artist mother's knee that in nature there is no pure black and no pure white, so you must always paint with shades of darkness, degrees of light.

Curiously, the dualistic myth of satanic evil has a counterpart, which we might call the myth of monistic goodness. It has been called "angelism," the view of human nature that denies (or does not take seriously) the reality of human finitude, failure, and fault. Finitude: we are limited and will die; failure: we make mistakes and "miss the mark" of our humanity; fault: we cannot entirely pass off our failings on others or on circumstances beyond our control without spiritually blinding ourselves, as did King Oedipus literally, to the truth. So dualism, taken in moderation, is not the problem.

Like "the poor you will always have with you," you will always have dualities with you, marking the yes and no of thought, the dark and light of perception, the "to be or not to be" of existential decision. It's not all that abstract. You will always need to make the twisted straight, starting with yourself. It's an imperative of our humanity; that is, it is something you cannot *not* do.

TEN

And he ordained twelve

Mark 3: 13-19 *And he goeth up into a mountain, and calleth unto him whom he would: and they came unto him. And he ordained twelve, that they should be with him, and that he might send them forth to preach, and to have power to heal sicknesses, and to cast out devils: And Simon he surnamed Peter; and James the son of Zebedee, and John the brother of James; and he surnamed them Boranerges, which is, The sons of thunder: and Andrew, and Philip, and Bartholemew, and Matthew, and Thomas, and James the son of Alphaeus, and Thaddaeus, and Simon the Canaanite, and Judas Iscaiot, which also betrayed him: and they went into his house.*

Jesus decides on twelve men, "whom he named apostles," to form his inner circle. They are authorized to preach and to "cast out demons." Theirs is a ministry to announce the present and coming rule of God in word and deed. Mark names them, and in some cases they are re-christened. Simon becomes Peter. John and James are called Boranerges, "which means sons of thunder"; they are twins as the nickname indicates. Then nine others are named, including another James (not Jesus' brother), and last of all Judas Iscariot, "who in fact betrayed him."

Speaking of the demonic, in my observation all churches are like this original church—they are betrayed from within.

It is noteworthy that Jesus did not work alone, and did not monopolize the preaching and healing authority he claimed for himself. Proclaiming the kingdom of God entailed giving these gifts away as quickly and widely as possible. And for this work he chose a devoted "band of brothers."

Did he choose only men? Scholars speculate that "the twelve" is a later invention of the early Church, wanting to style itself the New Israel with its own twelve tribes. Probably so, considering the obscurity of most of these guys. We often hear in the Gospels of a large number of followers, including women and, if women, also children. Everywhere in the Gospels Jesus himself seems to deal with women as easily and as sympathetically as with men. But it did not take long for patriarchal traditions to reassert themselves among his followers, so the tradition was formed that, just as there were twelve tribes of Israelites, headed by patriarchs, there must be twelve disciples, patriarchs all.

Peter comes first in the list of apostles. In Galilee, in northern Israel, I visited the Church of the Primacy of Peter, the first named among "the twelve"—ordained, Mark tells us, by Jesus himself. From the seed of this historical tradition, "the primacy of Peter," a mighty oak, the Catholic church, has grown. Mark, who does not claim to have been a disciple, is thought to have been a younger disciple of Peter. Perhaps he drew on Peter's memories when he sat down to write his Gospel—some forty years after the crucifixion of Jesus, at a time when eyewitnesses were being lost. It seems odd that, if Mark were closest to Peter, he does not report here or elsewhere the words of Jesus that Matthew reports following Peter's affirmation of Jesus as the Christ: "thou art Peter and upon this rock I will build my church" (Matthew 16: 18).

There is no evidence that Mark was an eye witness to the story he is telling, although some commentators have suggested he was the young man who escaped—without a stitch!—from Gethsemane. (See Mark 14: 51f.) Who else could have known this charming detail, and who could have thought to invent it? Of course, titillating speculations often gain more credence than they deserve.

ELEVEN
Behold my mother and my brethren!

Mark 3: 20-35 *And the multitude cometh together again, so that they could not so much as eat bread. And when his friends heard of it, they went out to lay hold on him: for they said, He is beside himself.*

And the scribes which came down from Jerusalem said, He hath Beelzebub, and by the prince of the devils casteth he out devils. And he called them unto him, and said unto them in parables, How can Satan cast out Satan? And if a kingdom be divided against itself, that kingdom cannot stand. And if a house be divided against itself, that house cannot stand. And if Satan rise up against himself, and be divided, he cannot stand, but hath an end. No man can enter into a strong man's house, and spoil his goods, except he will first bind the strong man; and then he will spoil his house. Verily I say unto you, All sins shall be forgiven unto the sons of men, and blasphemies wherewith soever they shall blaspheme: but they that shall blaspheme against the Holy Ghost hath never forgiveness, but is in danger of eternal damnation: Because they said, He hath an unclean spirit.

There came then his brethren and his mother, and, standing without, sent unto him, calling him. And the multitude sat about him, and they said unto him, Behold, thy mother and thy brethren without seek for thee. And he answered them, saying, Who is my mother, or my brethren? And he looked round about on them which sat about him, and said, Behold my mother and my brethren! For whosoever shall do the will of God, the same is my brother, and my sister, and my mother.

The passage is dense with events and words of significance. It requires us to bracket our family-friendly feelings about Mary and Joseph, and brothers and sisters. Mark implies that they are acting out of concern for Jesus, and ascribes the charge that he is possessed by Beelzebub, a major demon, to enemies who come down from the big city. Whatever his family think of this charge, he will not be called down by them, but names those about him, and whoever "does the will of God," as truly his mother, brother, and sister.

The assertion of the priority of religious community over family or clan loyalties has great historical significance. In a time when we are preoccupied with "the breakdown of the family," it is easy to forget that families can be stifling and clans can be oppressive, or even murderous. Giving priority to a faith community is one of the marks of a religion that accents conversion, issuing in the adoption of a new identity and sense of self. In consequence the early Christian community takes the form a voluntary association, and accordingly downgrades the involuntary associations of family, clan, tribe, and nation. It puts God before all these little Caesars.

"He... said to them through parables"—as usual! Here follows the saying about "a house divided." Again, he means to confute those who oppose him. Another parable follows, one that makes Mark's idea of Jesus' mission quite clear: first you have to bind the "strong man" (Satan), in his own house (the world); then you can "plunder his house." An equation is at work, here: as Satan possesses the world, so demons possess individual persons. The kingdom of God works at both levels. Mark does not shrink from ascribing strong, even violent imagery to the words of the supposedly "meek and mild" Jesus!

The "house divided" image, famously used by Abraham Lincoln to describe a "half-slave, half-free" United States, makes concrete one of the deeper recognitions of the interplay between good and evil in our experience: what is self-contradictory is self-negating, unstable, destined to fail. Theologian Paul Tillich interpreted self-contradiction ontologically, as a break-down in "the power of being" that is necessary for any existent being to sustain itself. When conflicts with others mask something deeper and more dangerous— psychic fissures, conflicts within ourselves—then *we* cannot stand.

These are not moral judgments—in fact, the gospel has moral implications but is not moralistic. What we have in this passage is a description of the human condition, words that tell us who we are.

Readers have often puzzled over the question: What is blasphemy "against the Holy Spirit," which Jesus calls the one unforgivable sin? Any sin or blasphemy can be forgiven, he says, except this. Mark explains that he said this "because they said he had an unclean spirit," a comment that directly follows his parables of a "house divided" and "binding the strong man." This cryptic explanation of a cryptic saying suggests that what is unforgiveable is deliberately to pervert the divine Spirit so that it becomes an evil spirit, a spirit that negates the very possibility of receiving the grace of forgiveness.

Doing wrong and knowing it is forgivable; doing wrong and not knowing it, then justifying and even exulting in it, is unforgivable because it is demonic. This is why our moral sensibilities count sincere remorse so heavily. What is unforgivable is our denial of any need to be forgiven, thus preventing moral release. In a curious way, the judgment is self-executing.

Here, as often seems the case, Jesus' words tell us more about the spiritual struggles we have with ourselves than they do about any distant realm of transcendence. With him transcendence is always present, near at hand, within our personal lives and experience. He was not a dreamy idealist but a radical realist.

"Unforgivable" may nevertheless sound too harsh, especially from one, like Jesus, who put so much stock in forgiveness. To think of "unforgivable" as a self-blinding willfulness, hence as a self-inflicted wound, removes it from the sense of moral judgment on others. The tragedy of king Oedipus, in Sophocles' play, is that he literally blinds himself to punish his metaphorical blindness; ironically, he loses literal sight and gains true "sight" at the same time. (We often ask after some great tragedy, did we have to go through that to learn better?) The truth Oedipus learns is the truth about himself; his redemption comes through a shock of self-recognition.

Who are we? We are the spirit that has come to dwell in us, either carrying us forward with grace and strength, or sometimes contorting us and even tearing us apart. This is a chief reason for prayer. To me Dante Alighieri's prayer, from the *Purgatorio*, is simple, profound, vivid, and memorable:

> *Give us this day our daily manna,*
> *without which, in this rough desert,*
> *they backward go who toil most to go on.*

The poet speaks in parables. However much we materially progress, if we are not fed "from above," as the Israelites were fed during their wilderness wanderings and Jesus was fed during his wilderness sojourn, we would spiritually and morally regress. We all need to ask, when do we withdraw enough from the world of "getting and spending, early and late," the world of unceasing toil, to let out souls be fed?

My colleague Laurel Hallman tells of being admonished by her mentor, Harry Schofield, "If you as a minister do not have a regular spiritual practice, you will dry up and blow away"—or so I remember her report. Her dialogues with Reverend Schofield and her reflections on the spiritual practices she developed are seen in the fine video she created, "Living by Heart." One practice is to save poems that speak to you in a special way, and sometimes commit them to memory. The goal of this spiritual practice is to live by heart. There is also the matter of Jesus' family. He is told they are "outside, looking for you." Family values do not seem to count for much in this account, and Jesus' attitude seems shockingly dismissive and callous. His mother and his brothers get all our sympathy. Precisely because the story doesn't seem like the kind Mark or his sources would make up, we may conclude that it contains a true historical memory.

I am reminded of the words of N. V. Lenin, upon hearing Beethoven's "Appassionato" piano sonata. He was deeply moved by this music, he said, but he could not allow himself to listen to it, lest it make him soft and sentimental! As we know, Lenin succeeded in stifling any tendencies toward humane feeling. Was Jesus less single-minded than the chief Bolshevik? Is my comparison any more offensive than Jesus' plain violation of the commandment to honor thy father and thy mother? As Ecclesiastes might have said: There is a time for sympathy, and a time for single-minded resolve.

It's often been remarked: See there? He had brothers! So if you're going to hang in there with the doctrine of the perpetual virginity of Mary, you're going to have to find some other explanation! And true believers always do. James Luther Adams tells the story of Harvard professor Kirsopp Lake at the vast Greek Orthodox monastery on Mt. Athos, where *no* female of *any* species was allowed to enter. One day the irreverent Lake espies a cat followed by a litter of kittens, and says to a chief monk: "See that? I thought no females were allowed here." The monk replies with a shrug, "That's no problem. It's a miracle."

Skeptics will say: See how believers fool themselves! I say: Belief in anything takes chutzpah, a refusal of helplessness and a denial of meaninglessness.

Authentic believing also recognizes that beliefs are expressed in symbols, not literal facts, such is the virginity of Mary, the mother of Jesus. How could she have several children and remain a virgin? A lot more miracles! I have said from time to time that the one and only miracle is spiritual freedom. But who can speak literally of something that is by definition indefinable? Parables, symbols, stories, and the like will be required; these are forms of resistance—refusals of helplessness and denials of meaninglessness.

Faith renews itself precisely in the face of resistance. That is what skeptics and scoffers regularly forget. *Faith renews itself in the face of resistance.*

TWELVE

The mystery of the kingdom of God

Mark 4: 1-20 *And he began again to teach by the sea side: and there was gathered unto him a great multitude, so that he entered into a ship, and sat in the sea; and the whole multitude was by the sea on the land. And he taught them many things by parables, and said unto them in his doctrine, Hearken; Behold, there went out a sower to sow; and it came to pass, as he sowed, some fell by the wayside, and the fowls of the air came and devoured it up. And some fell on stony ground, where it had not much earth; and immediately it sprang up, because it had no depth of earth: but when the sun was up, it was scorched; and because it had no root, it withered away. And some fell among thorns, and the thorns grew up, and choked it, and it yielded no fruit. And other fell on good ground, and did yield fruit that sprang up and increased: and brought forth, some thirty, and some sixty, and some an hundred. And he said unto them, He that hath ears to hear, let him hear.*

And when he was alone, they that were about him with the twelve asked of him the parable. And he said unto them, Unto you it is given to know the mystery of the kingdom of God: but unto them that are without, all these things are in parables: that seeing they may see, and not perceive; and hearing they may hear, and not understand; lest at any time they should be converted, and their sins should be forgiven them. And he said unto them, Know ye not this parable? And how then will ye know all parables?

The sower soweth the word. And these are they by the way side, where the word is sown; but when they have heard, Satan cometh immediately, and taketh away the word that was sown in their hearts. And these are they likewise which are sown on stony ground; who, when they have heard the word, immediately receive it with gladness; and have no root in themselves, and so endure not for a time: afterward, when affliction or persecution ariseth for the word's sake, immediately they are offended. And these are they which are sown among thorns; such as hear the word, and the cares of this world, and the decteitfulness of riches, and the lusts of other things entering in, choke the word, and it becometh unfruitful. And these are they which are sown on good ground; such as hear the word, and receive it, and bring forth fruit, some thirtyfold, some sixty, and some an hundred.

A small gem-like panel from his masterwork, *Maesta*, by the old master, Duccio (Sienna, c. 1255-1319), shows Jesus preaching from a boat to a multitude on the shore. This seemingly odd procedure has always caught the imagination of readers of the Gospels. In Herman Melville's *Moby Dick* Father Mapple preaches from a prow-shaped pulpit. Several times in the Gospel stories Jesus goes off on a boat, onto the Sea of Galilee, apparently in order to escape the crush of the crowds who gather wherever he appears. One reason for the crowding is the attempt to touch him, "even the hem of his garment." Preaching from a boat signals physical separation; it tells us, *this is no ordinary man, but a man apart.*

Mark's Jesus seems both entirely human and, at the same time, removed from ordinary humanity. Far from being a puppet in God's hands, he acts with an absolute independence, absolute resolve, absolute self-possession. Still, he appears as ordinary man, "a walking around Jesus," as John Updike calls Rembrandt's misty but humanized depictions, in contrast to El Greco's elongated and ethereal images of the Christ. In Mark he is by turns tremendously mysterious and entirely familiar. Then as now, some people respond to him with adulation and awe, others with hostility and fear.

The "parable of the sower" follows. This parable and its commentaries form a key to understanding Mark's "parabolic vision," his entire way of thought and speech.[20] Jesus himself tells us that it is a parable of parables: "And he said to them: You did not read [i. e., understand] this parable? Then how shall you understand all the [other] parables?" (Lattimore) The question sounds impertinent; again, Jesus appears exasperated by the density of his disciples. Parables are indeed something like jokes: if you get the point you laugh out loud, and if you don't you feel embarrassed. But clearly Mark and his friends were not content to leave it at that. So detailed interpretation follows. When the disciples ask Jesus what the parable of the sower means, he gives an allegorical explanation, purporting to show how each element of the story corresponds to a hidden meaning. The subject of this "parable of parables" turns out to be the causes of obscurity and incomprehension of his message. "The word," he explains, disseminated across the world, meets frequent failures and occasional, astonishing successes.

"Speaking in parables," then, does not make a message vivid or clear to everyone, but actually separates those on the *inside*, who understand, from those on the *outside*, who do not. It separates the spiritually living from the spiritually dead. It separates those who instantly know from those who are "invincibly ignorant." Max Weber, famous as a sociologist of religion, spoke of himself as "religiously unmusical." This thoroughly modern scholar was fascinated by religious ideas and practices, as his copious writings show, but confessed that he had little or no *personal* feeling for religion. The comment seems tinged with regret. Had I been Weber's counselor I might have said: *Herr professor, don't be so hard on yourself! For this little confession is a moment of humble self-reflection. "If you are lost enough to find yourself,"* as Robert Frost put it, *perhaps you are not lost after all!*

Many people feel they are uncomprehending and unfeeling outsiders to religion; would that they could awaken to the fact that this is our human condition, or so the parable of the sower tells us. This is the beginning of awakening itself.

Much ink has been spilled over questions of interpretation of the parable of the sower. Some have thought that Jesus himself is the sower and the seed he scatters is the Word, or perhaps the words, of God.

But we ask: Is this the way Mark understood the parable, whether or not Jesus so understood it? Perhaps, for this is what the allegorical interpretation that follows, ascribed to Jesus himself, suggests. Still, the details of the allegorical interpretation feel contrived; a reader begins to lose interest—just as we quickly lose interest when the teller of a joke tells why it is funny, or when a work of art is "authoritatively explained."

The three explanations for the failure of Jesus' word to take root with many listeners, are (1) falling prey to Satan, (2) not standing fast in the face of persecution, and (3) loving the things of this world too much. There is no explaining those who *do* prove fertile soil, and the abundance of their fruits, we are told, is immense.[21]

Here is my own allegorical interpretation for the parable's three kinds of "failure," correlating with them a moral typology: The hungry birds stand for *perversity*, the hard ground and hot sun stand for *moral weakness*, and the choking thorns stand for *self-seeking*. The opposites of these forms of spiritual failure are *faith, hope,* and *love,* traditionally called "theological virtues" and understood as foundational of all other virtues. These virtues taken together constitute a morally and spiritually fruitful life—like the seed falling on the good soil, growing up and producing an abundant crop. This is, to be sure, not exegesis; it is imaginative extrapolation. Nevertheless, it is one kind of seed planted by this seminal Gospel. Readers are hereby invited to generate their own imaginative allegories to explain the parable of the sower.

When the disciples ask Jesus about the meaning of the parable, he speaks of a gospel that is not only hidden from plain view, but *must* be hidden—an idea that shocks both piety and common sense. "To you are given the secret [*mysterion*] of the kingdom of God; but to those who are outside all comes through parables, so that they may have sight but not see, and hear but not understand, lest they be converted and forgiven." Why speak in parables? This turns the usual answer on its head, and commentators often flatly assert: Jesus can have said no such thing![2]

Perhaps, but the first task is to understand what Mark wrote. Asking whether the historical Jesus really said it comes second, and for good reason. If we leap too quickly to the second question, we increase the likelihood that we will discover the kind of Jesus we presupposed all along. The passage is hard to swallow because we think of parables as "sermon illustrations," meant to make ones point memorable and clear. But the passage reminds us that parables in Biblical usage are often "dark sayings," obscure oracles, or even riddles that only those specially gifted will be able to solve. John Bunyan quotes on the title page of *The Pilgrim's Progress* words of the prophet Hosea (12: 10): "I have used similitudes," giving Biblical precedent for his extravagant use of allegory. The King James Bible here uses "similitude" for *mashal*, the Hebrew word for parable, proverb, or allegory; the corresponding Greek word is *parabole*, literally meaning "to throw beside," hence a similitude. Mark's Jesus has not only antecedents in the Hebrew scriptures, but also descendents in the Gnostic understanding of the Gospel—an esoteric wisdom into which one must be initiated.

In this passage (Mark 4: 11-12) Jesus cites one of the most important passages in Hebrew scripture, the call and mission of the prophet Isaiah (Isa. 6: 9-10). This passage also underlies the *Sanctus* of the Catholic mass. In words invoking the unapproachable holiness of Yahweh, God's face is hidden by the wings of six cherubim, who cry *Sanctus, Sanctus, Sanctus*—Holy, Holy, Holy! Isaiah cannot prophesy for this unutterable holiness until his "unclean lips" are cleansed, seared by coals from the temple brazier.

The ancient Gnostics had a powerful image, explaining the spiritual deafness of humanity, an image that works even better in our age of super-amplification, "the noise of the world." As I read Isaiah 6, the prophet is told: Tell the people that the Word of God will be inaudible to them; in order to hear, they must somehow elude *the noise of the world*. There are many manifestations of the underlying spiritual principle, for instance: Before you can enjoy the abundance of the promised land, you must dwell in the wilderness and live on manna.

This, then, is the reason for speaking in parables. The world is opaque, alien, deafening, blinding, demonically possessed, deadly—any and all of the above! Before the holiness of God, the prophet is cast down for his sense of unworthiness, until his lips have been seared and purified; only then can he speak the Word that comes from the very mouth of God. Even then the world actively resists the prophetic

Word, which largely falls on deaf ears. And yet some good sprouts do spring up and grow to produce an abundance in the fullness of time.

We often hear that ours is "an age of science," so it is not surprising that scientism, the belief that all questions have scientific answers, is popular today. Owen Barfield, in his profound study of this contemporary form of idolatry, connects the words that Jesus quotes from Isaiah (Isa. 6: 9-10) to humanity's endemic devotion to products of its own imagination and manufacture: "We must hear sounding through these words [of Jesus] both the voice of the prophet Isaiah and the familiar voice of the Psalmist inveighing against graven images. We cannot do otherwise than read them as alluding to idolatry."[23] By "idols" Barfield means more than plaster statues or painted images; he means the kind of spiritual vanity that is described in the Book of Psalms:

> The idols of the heathen are silver and gold, the work of men's hands. They have mouths, but they speak not; eyes have they, but they see not; they have ears, but they hear not; neither is there any breath in their mouths. *They that make them are like unto them; so is every one that trusteth in them.* (Psalm 135: 15-18, KJV, italics added)

This is an observable phenomenon. The electronic game industry claims that "studies" (the only test of truth in our "age of science") have not demonstrated that videogames involving participation in repetitive acts of imagined violence are harmful to children. The preoccupation to the point of addiction seen in children who spend hour after hour with these intensely engaging instruments of learning suggests otherwise. Or do we believe that education has no significant moral effect on growing minds?

Mark's Jesus minces no words: "... but for those outside everything is in parables; *so that* they may indeed see but not perceive, and may indeed hear but not understand; lest they should turn again and be forgiven" (Mark 4: 12, Lattimore). Frank Kermode notes that Mark's Greek word *hina* ("so that" or "in order that"), was altered in Matthew's parallel passage to the Greek word *hoti* ("because" –see Matthew 13: 13). Matthew's version suggests that Jesus speaks in parables *because* the people are without understanding and need help—and if they still don't comprehend, it is their own failure.

Apparently, the difficulty of this passage was felt virtually from the outset, with the result that Matthew, whose Gospel follows and expands Mark's, reinterprets this notoriously "hard saying" of Jesus. Ironically, Matthew's version is softer on Jesus than Mark's, and harder on his listeners! Mark's *hina* ("in order that") puts the onus on Jesus himself: he tells parables *in order that* they, the "outsiders," *shall remain uncomprehending outsiders.* In "Directive" Robert Frost captures Mark's meaning with perfect pitch. The poem's setting is Vermont in early spring. Its mountain-hiking pilgrim, one who is "lost enough to find himself," keeps in a place known only to himself "a broken drinking goblet"—actually a child's cup—"like the Grail / Under a spell so the wrong ones can't find it, / So can't get saved, as Saint Mark says they mustn't." The last line sums up the spiritual "directive" of the poem: "Drink and be whole again beyond confusion."[24]

What do I make of Mark's obscure and fascinating passage? To my understanding the gospel is a spiritual power hidden within the world, although I am mostly too "full of myself" to find it, and finding it, too proud to drink of it. The gospel is about transformation, an inward turning that opens the heart outward to others—a losing your self in order to find yourself—a being innocent enough to "taste and see," as the Psalmist bids us, the goodness of the creation and its Creator.

The gospel is not a road map, for we must choose our own pathways, but precisely a "directive" to reclaim our spiritual wholeness, our salvation. "Salvation" is derived from the Latin, *salvare,* consonant with many terms that are like it: saving and salutary, hale and healthy, whole and holy, integral and integrity. In one sense these qualities of being are gifts, pure and simple; in another sense we must lay claim to them, if we would possess them. The active and the passive are connected, as are the expressive and the receptive; they are not opposites but polarities on a continuum.

The odd little word that Kermode calls attention to, *hina,* has powerful spiritual implications. "In order that" carries with it a "hard intentionality," as we are likely to feel when we are directed to forgive others *in order that* we may be forgiven. This may seem self-serving, the opposite of virtuous disinterest. In fact it strikes at the root of self-righteousness—an unblinking belief in our own moral superiority. We often hear about "unconditional love" as the highest moral ideal; I'm not against it, but it sounds a little other-worldly and in need of a measure of real-world "tough love." Is "love in order that you may be loved" cold calculation? Or is it real-world realism, bracing but true? Here again, the gospel has a unfamiliar objectivity; it says, be what you intend *in order that* the realm of God-ruling may be visible.

The famous prayer attributed to St. Francis of Assisi also links moral cause and effect, inviting if not quite stating a similar "hard intentionality": "For it in giving that we receive; it is in pardoning that we are pardoned; and it is in dying that we are born to eternal life." The Lord's Prayer, too, reminds us of the moral linkage between giving and receiving. They are as cause and effect: "Forgive us our debts, as we also have forgiven our debtors" (Matthew 6: 12). Neither *hoti* (because) nor *hina* (in order that) occurs here, but the latter hina, is implied: Forgive your debtors if you want to be forgiven your debts!

"Debts" may be a better translation than "trespasses," because debts arise from transactions: repayment is a moral obligation, but debts can also be forgiven, which is to say, cancelled. This clarifies the meaning of forgiveness: To be forgiven is to be released from a moral obligation or a penalty that is owed. Plato's idea of *methexis* (participation)—his central belief that particular beings are expressions of universal and transcendent forms—helps us understand the imperative another way: *Participate in the realm of forgiveness, both forgiving and being forgiven, and in the reality of spiritual freedom, both liberating and being liberated.*

THIRTEEN
Take heed what ye hear

Mark 4:21-29 *And he said unto them, Is a candle brought to be put under a bushel, or under a bed? And not to be set on a candlestick? For there is nothing hid, which shall not be manifested; neither was any thing kept secret, that it should come abroad. If any man have ears to hear, let him hear. And he said unto them, Take heed what ye hear; with what measure ye mete, it shall be measured to you; and unto you that hear shall more be given. For he that hath, to him shall be given: and he that hath not, from him shall be taken even that which he hath.*

And he said, So is the kingdom of God, as if a man should cast seed into the ground; and should sleep, and rise night and day, and the seed should spring and grow up, he knoweth not how. For the earth bringeth forth fruit of herself: first the blade, then the ear, after that the full corn in the ear. But when the fruit is brought forth, immediately he putteth in the sickle, because the harvest is come.

Having instructed us on the nature of parables, several parables follow in rapid succession. The first concerns the lamp that is intended to give light and not to be hidden, tells us that the secret of the kingdom of God will not be secret forever: "for there is nothing hidden except to be shown, nor anything concealed except to be brought to light"—

nicely saying the same thing twice, as Hebrew poetry regularly does. I may deal in obscurities, Jesus is saying, but they will not be obscure forever or I wouldn't be doing it. Expectation is everything.

Expectation reminds us that the time is not ripe, that "now" is still a looming "not yet." Something is being held off, as with the infamous prayer that Saint Augustine recalled from his youth: "Lord, make me chaste, but not yet!" The *ripeness* of time, the *fullness* of time, the *appointed* time, the *kairos*—this (apologies to Shakespeare) is such stuff as the gospel is made on. Life itself is like that—being lived toward the future, it needs to be lived by faith. It is an obscurity, even a secret withheld from us; but perhaps not forever. It is like Saint Paul's parable of the distorting mirror in which *now* we see only puzzling reflections ("for now we see through a glass, darkly"), but *then* we shall see "face to face," and "know as also we are known" (1 Corinthians 13: 13). These eschatological words bring with them a felt shudder, a humbling quiet, a longing to be at peace.

Paul Ricoeur speaks of reading Biblical texts not for what "lies behind" them—as if to root out the true meaning by an archeological dig—but to read them for what comes into view "in front" of them. We can only live *forward* in time. Our interest in the text is not, finally, the experience from which it came, but the life, the activity, the "way of being in the world" toward which it directs us. Ricoeur's thought is continuously complex, but this sentence plainly captures his idea: "A text… is like a musical score in that it requires execution."[25] Silently rereading *The Iliad* recently, I thought: How wonderful it would be to hear a bard perform this text, *intone it,* as it was intended! With such a recitation I can imagine myself inhabiting a world as distant as Homer's, for those who people his story are readily recognizable today. Homer, too, frequently spoke in parables—usually called similes—and like Jesus drew upon keen observation of every-day experience. A beautiful example is Paieon's miraculous healing of the battle-wounds of Ares:

> As when the juice of the fig in white milk rapidly fixes
> That which was fluid before and curdles quickly for one who
> Stirs it; in such speed as this he healed violent Ares.[26]

Insofar as Mark's text is like a musical score, requiring *lived* performance, his Gospel is eschatological throughout: it constantly evokes a world, a time and a place of expectation, that with the gift of faith we might inhabit. Emily Dickinson:

> A word is dead when it is said, some say,
> I say it just begins to live that day.

This world is familiar: the lamp belongs not under a bushel or a bed (the old *reductio ad absurdum*) but on a lamp-stand where it will give light to all in the house. To believe that the lamp will be put in its proper place becomes an image of the way darkness is banished, namely, by putting a source of light to its intended use. The meaning of the text lies in its "performance," that is, its enactment. God, the true intent of all our fallible and short-sighted intentionality, is the One who brings the truth to light—the One who puts the lamp to its intended use, "to give light to all in the house."

The words are characteristic of Jesus: "He who has ears to hear, let him hear." This implies that many do not have ears capable of "hearing." Jesus did not preach "positive thinking": he often speaks of the failure to hear, to understand, and to respond his message. Capability is a matter of power, and power is double-edged. Education illustrates what this means: All people are somewhat educated, for our very humanity depends on the capacity to learn; however, to be relatively uneducated is to be relatively powerless. To recognize this is to affirm education as a human right.

We usually think of power as the capacity to influence, as "power over," and in this negative sense, threats are powerful. Power also underlies our word "potentiality," a latent capacity. The idea of empowerment is rooted in the ancient Greek idea of *dynamis* (power), from which we get the word "dynamic." In Plato's two-edged understanding, power is equally the capacity to affect and to be affected. (See Plato, *Sophist* 248c). To be empowered is to participate in a force larger than ourselves; we must receive it in order to be able to express it. Just so, *not* "to have ears to hear" is to be powerless. Being incapable of receiving, we are incapable of giving.

In this mode of being, this double vision, I must forever question myself: Am I able to hear? If not, how can I speak? (Children who cannot hear do not learn to speak; adults who talk and rarely listen have forgotten where they came from.) The power to make is a gift we are given—a *charism*, grace. In fact, we are ourselves made, mysteriously knit in our mother's womb. What greater gift than to be given being and life? Those who deny the gift or imagine that it is no gift, may fashion themselves "self-made men"; they tend, then, to deaden humane impulses.

Jesus goes straight on to utter a warning: "Consider what you hear." He lays out a conundrum that apparently snagged Shakespeare's restless imagination, resulting in his almost-mythic play, *Measure for Measure*. In the play Angelo (*i.e.*, humanity), who is given rule of Vienna (*i. e.*, the world) in the absence of the prince (*i. e.*, God), proves himself not "a little less than the angels" (Psalm 8: 5) but far less! Things get so bad that the play could easily have been a tragedy, but in the end "the measure [Angelo] gives is the measure [Angelo] gets," (*i. e.*, his just desserts), so it turns out to be a morality play.

I understand Jesus' words as follows: "Your measure [your righteousness in the sight of God] will be made by the measure with which you measure [the righteousness of your own life], and more shall be added to you" [rather like "incentivized giving"]. In other words: righteousness is its own reward, and unrighteousness, its own punishment; as a result: "When a man has, he shall be given; when one has not, even what he has shall be taken away from him" (Mark 4: 25, Lattimore translation). What? Is Robin Hood to steal from the poor and give to the rich? The words turn our native sense of justice upside down. Many commentators scratch their heads over what seems perverse and conclude that Jesus can have said no such thing. I understand it this way: *Righteousness* is not something we are given as a reward for good behavior; it is something we either *have* or *have not*; it is a potency that either grows abundantly, or else withers and dies. How, then, do we appropriate righteousness?

Here again the exegetical principle is operative: "hard sayings" are the more likely to be authentic precisely because nobody would have made them up. "Authentic" is an equivocal word, in any event: we are interested in the text itself, the document that has come into being and has exercised its seminal power by virtue of capturing a life that once appeared, if only as a camera records a series of snapshots. The saying is consonant with the parable of the sower. It is also consonant with the ideas that rewards and punishments are proportional to deeds, for we live in a world of consequences.

Hard sayings induce mental wrestling, for instance, in this case, reminding us of a scrap of worldly wisdom, "Them that got, gets." It even suggests that God is the author of this *dis*proportionate justice. Of course, it makes a great deal of difference what commodity is being distributed. Those who are somehow given the capacity to hear, to receive, and to respond will hear more, respond more, and be more. And those who are, for whatever reason, tragically incapable of hearing and receiving and speaking, they will be disempowered all the more. It's as if a God-given power, a divine *dynamis* that flows and ebbs in our lives, were the stuff of authentic living.

A troubling question lurks at the edges of these reflections: Human beings may be more ethical, in the sense of just and compassionate, than a God who apparently affords us grossly disproportionate rewards. (There is always a tension between the idea of God as benevolent and God as powerful. Is God goodness writ large, or "a consuming fire"?)

We are also active agents in the handling of the "stuff" of authentic living— a crude phrase, but apt enough if its quantity is to be measured by the cupful. Our measure will be taken by the truthfulness, the righteousness, the guilelessness of our measuring—our "purity of heart" (Matthew 5: 8). Again, as with my previous remarks on Mark's use of *hina*, "in order that," we are surprised to learn that our own intent counts so heavily. To be judged by the way we make judgments is daunting. "What should we do?" we ask. It's a moment Jean Paul Sartre would relish, for he would say: Lay claim to your freedom and decide for yourself. This is not at all like standing before a cosmic judge, or even a loving parent; we are not finally judged by standards that may or may not be fully spelled out. It is more like being invited to write your own rulebook in "the great game of life." Except that it's not really a game; more nearly it is what Emily Dickinson called the "most profound experiment / appointed unto men."

We can imagine Mark as a collector and organizer of sayings and stories of Jesus more readily than we can imagine Jesus knocking out these gem-like parables in rapid order. In any event Jesus proceeds on a more positive note. The much-loved parable of "the seed growing secretly" affirms the abundant spiritual harvest that the kingdom of God brings without the slightest effort on our part. Better, we could say that God "sets the stage" (Shakespeare) or "prepares the table" (Psalm 23) or "arranges the rendezvous" (Wallace Stevens) for us. Here again the parable sounds a note of urgency: The abundance will rot in the fields unless timely action is taken, so put in the sickle "for the time of harvesting has come." God offers, but we must be ready and willing to act when the time is ripe.

The parable suggests, then, that God "offers" when the appointed hour, the *kairos*, has come. A soft-boiled egg may take four minutes to cook to my taste, but when it comes to actually cooking this egg, the four-minute bell marks the *kairos:* get it out of the water now! English makes no verbal distinction between the two kinds of time, so we may say: Well, time is time, so it's really all the same." The word "really" often betrays a bias in favor of the "objective" viewpoint, looking at something from the outside, as an object over against the observing subject. Shakespeare understood the difference: "There is a tide in the affairs of men, which, taken at the flood leads on... ." Internal, subjective time is different from external, objective time. Saint Augustine recognized that time has a profound but elusive religious significance; through lengthy meditations in his *Confessions* he concluded that time is an expression of our internal, not our external, clocks—our impassioned organisms, not our well-devised mechanisms.[27] Augustine has been called the discoverer of human personality, due to his intensely introspective autobiographical story; he displays his humanity by becoming one who stands over against an inscrutable yet intimately related God. This is why his *Confessions* take the form of an extended series of personal prayers, making it one of the most influential books written.

Our lives are ordered by our bodily rhythms, moving within the rhythms of the day, the season, the life-time, and conscious also of epochs and the awkward shifts from one age to another. It has become fashionable to speak of our age as "post-modern," not really knowing what that means; no wonder, for the word itself gives us no clue, except to say that our time comes after something else. Yet perhaps there is a clue in our very negation. For to define ourselves in contrast to what has gone before is still to define ourselves, to mark ourselves off from what is not ourselves. We must mean by this phrase, "after-the-modern-age," an age that stands both in continuity with and in discontinuity from the age that has gone before. Jesus' announcement of a kingdom *that is coming* and fulfills *what has been long prepared* follows similar lines of thought. He moves us to ask the eschatological question: What comes after this?

To enter into dialogue is to recognize that *you* are not *I*, but *an other* person, and yet: *I am like you at least in this, that we can speak to one another*—we can "have ears to hear." Personality, identity, and consciousness are concepts that point to the same hard-to-grasp inner reality. Nothing pursues me more relentlessly, or so Emily Dickinson attests in the concluding stanza of her poem, "This consciousness that is aware"—

> Adventure most unto itself
> The Soul condemned to be—
> Attended by a single Hound
> Its own identity.[28]

Our identity is something that pursues us as relentlessly as a hound, perhaps "the hound of heaven." Just this, the poem tells, is the "most profound experiment" to which we are "appointed." This feels Kafkaesque: The experiment assigned to us and impossible to evade is the discovery of our own unique identity. Consciousness of this life-task pursues us on and on. We run before it, aware that our chronological time is finite, and yet, we pray, our *kairos*, our fulfillment, touches infinity.

FOURTEEN

What manner of man is this?

Mark 4: 30-41 *And he said, Whereunto shall we liken the kingdom of God? Or with what comparison shall we compare it? It is like a grain of mustard seed, which, when it is sown in the earth, is less than all the seeds that be in the earth: But when it is sown, it growth up, and becometh greater than all herbs, and shooteth out great branches; so that the fowls of the air may lodge under the shadow of it. And with many such parables spake he the word unto them, as they were able to hear it. But without a parable spake he not unto them: and when they were alone, he expounded all things to his disciples.*

And the same day, when the even was come, he saith unto them, Let us pass over unto the other side. And when they had sent away the multitude, they took him even as he was in the ship. And there arose a great storm of wind, and the waves beat into the ship, so that it was now full. And he was in the hinder part of the ship, asleep on a pillow; and they awake him, and say unto him, Master, carest thou not that we perish? And he arose, and rebuked the wind, and said unto the sea, Peace, be still. And the wind ceased, and there was a great calm. And he said unto them, Why are ye so fearful? How is it that ye have no faith? And they feared exceedingly, and said one to another, What manner of man is this, that even the wind and the sea obey him?

Last in this series of Jesus' famous and familiar mini-parables of the kingdom of God comes "the mustard seed." It speaks of astonishing and delightful transformation, and even the birds make nests in its boughs! This smallest-to-largest transformation sounds more literary than literal. Are mustard seeds really so small, and their plants really so large? No matter; we don't forget the parable.

Effective teachers often use hyperbole. The greatest exemplar of this method in my experience was Paul Tillich, whose grand generalizations and fanciful assertions produced that most precious commodity, insight. For instance: "The half-smile of Greek sculptures of the archaic period," he said, "is the smile that anticipates the coming of a great classical period." And we smile at the very thought of this hyperbolic thought.

"Tell a lie, and then qualify it," was George Lyman Kittredge's method for effective pedagogy, or so James Luther Adams remembered from his Shakespeare classes, over which Kittredge presided as one with authority. For instance, when a student started hacking during a lecture he would pause and bark out, "Stop it! Just stop it!" and the coughing would stop. Kittredge held that coughing in class was no more than "a personal indulgence."

The parable of the mustard seed reinforces our dominant impression that the gospel is all about transformation, all about astonishment and awakening. Paul Tillich spoke of *agape*, the New Testament word for self-giving love in "mustard seed" terms; he said that *agape* is "love that cares for the smallest without itself becoming small."[29] Neither did Tillich ignore *eros*, averring, for instance that "the good thing about pornography" was that it extended sexuality into old age. Do I have your attention? Need I now qualify the thought?

"But he did not talk with them except in parables" (Lattimore translation). The King James Version's is more elegant, "But without a parable spake he not unto them." The meaning is the same. Suppose we take Mark at his word: *everything* Jesus said was in parables, *nothing* was in plainspoken expository prose, with stories and metaphors added for rhetorical spice. The statement, found only in Mark, seems extraordinary, even if it refers only to his "teachings," words of significant import. (Obviously Mark did not include matter-of-fact comments, such as, "Please pass the wine.") It raises other questions in our minds, as well: What of the stories of healings and exorcisms—which often seem to be teaching stories—in which the lesson ("the moral of the story") seems more important than the event being narrated? And just what is a parable? A this-is-like-that story? But if *that* is never explained in standard expository prose we are left with a riddle or a dark saying; "the point" is never explained and we may be left to "get it" on our own. "Getting it" seems to be a kind of insight, a sudden recognition, or a revelation.

Mark goes on to say that "privately with his own disciples he expounded all," as if the inner circle were given privileged communications—even though elsewhere they continue to seem dolts, even though this contradicts our notion of Jesus ministering equally to all who came his way. Why the secrecy? Why the riddling parables? And why, according to Mark, does he speak *only in parables*?

"We miss what is unique about Biblical faith," Paul Ricoeur writes, "if we take categories such as narrative, oracle, commandment, and so on as rhetorical devices that are alien to the content they transmit. What is admirable, on the contrary, is that structure and *kerygma* [proclaimed message] accommodate each other in each form of narration."[30] Opening "the secret of the kingdom of God" is not a matter of grasping some ancient and obscure scrap of wisdom, something so esoteric that only those who hold the correct interpretive key can unlock its meaning. It is more nearly an event, something we grasp in the moment that we are grasped by it. This is why Jesus' teaching is of a piece with his acts of healing. His healings are effected by eliciting words of faith from those who suffer. Likewise his preaching is of a piece with his exorcisms, for both are constituted by words that affect us deeply. Likewise his message is of a piece with his miracles, for both evoke the sense of living in a new world of possibility.

All these words and deeds are expressions of what Kenneth Burke calls "symbolic action," the third wonder of his "three great wonders" of existence. The first great wonder, Burke says, is sheer being, leading us to ask, why is there something rather than nothing? The second great wonder is the capacity of *some* beings for growth and replication, in other words, living beings. The third great wonder, the one most proper to us as human beings, is *symbolic action*, for instance, language, art, music, dance, and mathematics. The human capacity for producing meanings and purposes, for "calling to mind" both the world we are fated to inhabit and the world we choose to inhabit, are expressions that constitute the forms of symbolic action.[31]

The Gospel of Mark is alive with symbolic action. Through its tapestry of teachings and stories, it calls up a world that is both fated and chosen. What kind of a world is it? A world that remains opaque to all eyes but the eyes of faith. That is the reason for teaching in parables, to solve the riddle. Vladimir Nabokov observed, "The unraveling of a riddle is the purest and most basic act of the human mind."[32]

This section of Mark (chapter 4) ends where it began, perhaps by design: Jesus is on a boat, again escaping the crushing crowd. Again he is with his disciples, who once again go unnamed, suggesting that they may actually have been a motley crew of men, women, and children. He sleeps while a violent storm lashes the boat, and is awakened only by his tremulous disciples: "Master, do you not care whether we perish?" The scene is reminiscent of Jonah, but unlike Jonah, Jesus is not fleeing his prophetic mission, and he is not thrown overboard by the nervous sailors. Rather, Jesus says they would not be afraid if they had faith, and silences the storm with three words: "Silence, be still." He is able to still the storm because he does have faith, the hallmark of which is *living without fear*.

Nothing is said of Jesus having magical powers; in fact, here as in other miracle stories faith is accented precisely to preclude the thought that Jesus practiced magic. Yet it is a miracle big enough to cause the disciples, in an ironic twist, *really* to be afraid. "Who is this," they say to one another, "that even the wind and the sea obey him?" It is not his power to still the storm but what that power says about him that frightens them.

Is this a miracle story or another parable, a teaching story in which the storm has a symbolic meaning? It is possible that Mark did not draw any such distinction. All events with supernatural import are events with symbolic import.

I'm reminded of the story of the little boy who comes into his parents' room at night and says, "Daddy! Mommy! There's a bear in my room!" "Never mind," his father says, "it's not real." "I know," the boy says, "that's why I'm afraid of it!"

The disciples want Jesus to work his magic to save them from drowning; he wants them to discover the faith that stills the violent storm of our existence. Shakespeare, in his valedictory play, "The Tempest," draws on the same symbolic meanings: the human condition is marked by our inner tempests, dramatically displayed for us by the artist-magician, Prospero, who both conjures up and resolves its mingled hopes and fears.

The message is at one with the miracle. But what is a miracle? It is something that amazes us because we cannot explain it, and delights us because it is wonderful and we did not expect it. We only confuse ourselves with arguments about the impossibility of contradicting the laws of natural science. The laws of nature partake of Kenneth Burke's "first great wonder," and as such are miracles in their own right; if they were not, we ourselves would not be! What, then, is the *message* of Mark's story of Jesus stilling the storm?

When I sailed a glassy-calm Sea of Galilee on the "Jesus Boat," one bright Sunday morning a few years ago, I led a brief Sunday service with my fellow-travelers. The Isareli boat captain said that this was the very spot where Jesus stilled the storm, so I took the tale as my homily's text. It also fit our emotional context. Having traveled the roads of Palestine and sympathetically felt the rage and fear of the people living under an endless military occupation, I bid my companions still the storm in their hearts, as Jesus stilled the storm on these very waters. We need not let go of righteous anger in the face of injustice, but we do need to temper anger with reason, with clarity of intent, with good will for all people. That would seem to me the kind of miracle we are looking for.

Do I dodge what seems obvious in Mark's story, that Jesus had power over natural forces, even the wind and the sea, while the disciples still thought of him only as their teacher? Let me answer the question with another question: if he really "did not speak without a parable," isn't his command, "Silence! Be still," also a parable, a story with a meaning extending beyond its original context? As for history—literal, factual history, untouched by human interest—no one can say what happened that day and in the last analysis it's beside the point.

The disciples ask, What manner of man is this? We answer, he is the parable-teller whose life, whose words and deeds, have become a parable, a story that "reveals a world we might inhabit."

FIFTEEN

My name is Legion

Mark 5: 1-20 *And they came over unto the other side of the sea, into the country of the Gadarenes. And when he was come out of the ship, immediately there met him out of the tombs a man with an unclean spirit, who had his dwelling among the tombs; and no man could bind him, no, not with chains: because that he had been often bound with fetters and chains, and the chains had been plucked asunder by him, and the fetters broken in pieces; neither could any man tame him. And always, night and day, he was in the mountains, and in the tombs, crying, and cutting himself with stones. But when he saw Jesus afar off, he ran and worshipped him, and cried with a loud voice, and said, What have I to do with thee, Jesus, thou Son of the most high God? I adjure thee by God, that thou torment me not. For he said unto him, Come out of the man, thou unclean spirit. And he asked him, What is thy name? And he answered, saying, My name is Legion: for we are many. And he besought him much that he would not send them away out of the country. Now there was there nigh unto the mountains a great herd of swine feeding. And all the devils besought him, saying, Send us into the swine, that we may enter into them. And forthwith Jesus gave them leave. And the unclean spirits went out, and entered into the swine: and the herd ran violently down a steep place into the sea, (they were about two thousand;) and were choked in the sea. And they that fed the swine fled, and told* *it in the city, and in the country. And they went out to see what it was that was done. And they came to Jesus, and see him that was possessed with the devil, and had the legion, sitting, and clothed, in his right mind: and they were afraid. And they saw it told them how it befell to him that was possessed with the devil, and also concerning the swine. And they began to pray him to depart out of their coasts. And when he was come into the ship, he that had been possessed with the devil prayed him that he might be with him. Howbeit Jesus suffered him not, but saith unto him, Go home to thy friends, and tell them how great things the Lord hath done for thee, and hath had compassion on thee. And he departed, and began to publish in Decapolis how great things Jesus had done for him: and all men did marvel.*

Here is the amazing story of Jesus' and "the Gerasene demoniac," the fierce and frightful man who mutilates himself and roams among the tombs, where the restless spirits of the dead roam also, seeking some body to possess. Jesus transfers them, over their shrieked protests, to a herd of swine, who are crazed and plunge into the sea, where they drown. There is no suggestion that the man himself is evil, or is in any wise a great sinner. When he speaks demons seem to be speaking through him; he is not himself, but a multitude of selves. Roman legions had 3000 to 6000 foot soldiers and cavalry. Even after being rid of the demons he is not rechristened, but remains "Legion." It would seem that this was never so much a name as a state of being, a compulsive, possessed state of being "beside himself." Thanks to Jesus' compassionate exorcism he has "come to himself," is "at one with himself," or we may say has become again a "centered self" (Paul Tillich's term) and self-reliant (Ralph Waldo Emerson's ideal). Compassion effects transformation, from being possessed to self-possession.

Mark charms us with his seeming lack of sophistication. It's the odd details that fascinate, such as the demons crying out, "I adjure you, before God, do not torment me." Even demons, it seems, cry out for mercy, all the while they recognize what ordinary mortals do not: that their "tormenter" is "Jesus, the son of the most high God." How painful it is to let go of our demons! How they howl from our very throats in protest!

Here as so often in Mark Jesus moves in a world torn by malevolent spiritual forces, not unlike our 21st century world. He acts to establish calm, balance, sanity, peace, as we should also. Just don't expect gratitude. Rather than rejoice, the people are frightened by this astonishing exorcism—almost as if they dared not hope to see such a healing power among them.

Jesus' ministry is a ministry of compassion. It's curious, I think, that his own involvement in the dark world of demonic powers goes hand in hand with his involvement in the pitiful world of human suffering. So this too is a teaching story: go and do likewise. If you would do good, do not expect to keep your hands clean—or keep your popularity in the neighborhood, for that matter. You will deal with pigs. When the demons implore him for a new abode in the swine, we are told quite simply, "He consented." Jonathan Edwards spoke of "consent to being," the fundamental attitude of the heart that is moved by God.[33] Even the demons belong to God, and implore God for compassion.

Belief in demons is supposedly something that enlightened people don't do any more. Then they may read a book called *All the Devils Are Here*, about the making of the global financial disaster that began in 2008 and affects us all still today.[34] The book chronicles the culture of greed that came to infect a large array of men and women deemed too prestigious to be prosecuted for crimes. Shakespeare's line from *The Tempest* provides the perfect *Schadenfreude*, "Hell is empty and all the devils are here," conjuring the whole cast of characters who found themselves dancing among the financial tombs of America. And "too big to jail."

The man who had been Legion and is now at one with himself begs Jesus to let him go with him. He wants to stay close to him, clinging to his savior. People have always fallen in love with their therapists. Psychotherapists don't let themselves get sucked in, but exercise "tough love," as does Jesus, sending the man off to live without neurotic dependency. (I owe this interpretation to a wise and compassionate counselor, William Hawley, in Austin, Texas.) To be well is also to cut your apron strings and be free, not only from outward but also from inner constraints—that is, not only physical and social but also psychic and spiritual constraints.

SIXTEEN

But the woman fearing and trembling

Mark 5: 21-43 *And when Jesus was passed over again by ship unto the other side, much people gathered unto him: and he was nigh unto the sea. And, behold, there cometh one of the rulers of the synagogue, Jairus by name; and when he saw him, he fell at his feet, and besought him greatly, saying, My little daughter lieth at the point of death: I pray thee, come and lay thy hands on her, that she may be healed; and she shall live. And Jesus went with him; and much people followed him, and thronged him.*

And a certain woman, which had an issue of blood twelve years, and had suffered many things of many physicians, and had spent all that she had, and was nothing bettered, but rather grew worse, when she had heard of Jesus, came in the press behind, and touched his garment. For she said, If I may touch but his clothes, I shall be whole. And straightway the fountain of her blood was dried up; and she felt in her body that she was healed of that plague. And Jesus, immediately knowing in himself that virtue had gone out of him, turned him about in the press, and said, Who touched my clothes? And his disciples said unto him, Thou seest the multitude thronging thee, and sayest thou, Who touched me? And he looked round about to see her that had done this thing. But the woman fearing and trembling, knowing what was done in her, came and fell down before him, and told him all the truth. And he said unto her, Daughter, thy faith hath made thee whole; go in peace, and be whole of thy plague.

While yet he spake, there came from the ruler of the synagogue's house certain which said, thy daughter is dead: why troublest thou the Master any further? As soon as Jesus heard the word that was spoken, he saith unto the ruler of the synagogue, Be not afraid, only believe. And he suffered no man to follow him, save Peter, and James, and John the brother of James. And he cometh to the house of the ruler of the synagogue, and seeth the tumult, and them that wept and wailed greatly. And when he was come in, he saith unto them, Why make ye this ado, and weep? The damsel is not dead but sleepeth.

And they laughed him to scorn. But when he had put them all out, he taketh the father and the mother of the damsel, and them that were with him, and entereth in where the damsel was lying. And he took the damsel by the hand, and said unto her, TALITHA CUMI; which is, being interpreted, Damsel, I say unto thee, arise. And straightway the damsel arose, and walked; for she was of the age of twelve years. And they were astonished with a great astonishment. And he charged them straitly that no man should know it; and commanded that something should be given her to eat.

Lattimore's translation is no different in meaning but is easier for us to take in: "And the woman, in fear and trembling, knowing what had happened to her, threw herself down before him and told him the whole truth." If you can place yourself in the drama of this one sentence, you cannot not know that this text is potent and fruitful. Some commentators have noted the prominence of women in Mark's Gospel; in fact, they see a symbolic pattern, with thirteen (twelve plus one) women, of whom the woman with a flow of blood and "the damsel" who had died, are two. Alice Lane, a colleague in ministry, writes: "Jesus' action toward the woman with the hemorrhage is all the more upsetting to the existing order and social mores of his time as Jesus attends to one who is ritually unclean, one who has been an outcast for twelve years. He does not recoil from her, but praises her faith, calls her 'daughter,' honoring her, and bids her to go in peace."[35]

Here, then, are two healing stories. One is the story of the woman who had suffered a "flow of blood," apparently a menstrual bleeding, for many years. This story interrupts the other story, which tells of Jesus raising of the twelve-year-old daughter of Jarius from the dead. Are these stories linked by concern for the restoration of womanly fertility? Mark gives no such hint and apparently is only passing on traditions as he has received them. That these stories are rooted in the time and place of Jesus and his first followers seems attested by the Aramaic words with which Jesus calls the young girl to arise, *Talitha cumi!*

Each has a detail that makes it memorable—even unforgettable. The story of the hemorrhaging woman gives us the phrase, to "touch the hem of his garment." (Matthew adds "hem" to Mark's version.) That the woman approaches from behind accents that Jesus did not see her coming, but only notices when he feels "power" flow out of him, stanching the blood that flows out of her. Thus he heals unconsciously, but here again, only on account of her faith. After all, if everyone who touched his garments in this sweaty, crowded environment got a jolt, he would be virtually "shorted out." Yes, we do get the impression that his healing power is something as palpable as an electrical current. The Polynesians and Melanesians call it *mana*, "the power of elemental forces of nature embodied in a person or a thing."

Must a believer take every healing story literally? A "true believer," perhaps so, but not a garden variety believer, I think. Speaking personally, I would be loathe to part with such stories. It is not just that to do so puts my own judgment above that of a text made sacred by the devotion of so many generations. Nor is it just that symbolic meanings may lie within reported events, as we see even in these seemingly literal tales. Beyond either of these end-runs around literalism, there is this, more deeply felt consideration: These stories give unadorned testimony to the very stuff of our desperation and hope, our "hope against hope" in times of dire suffering and need. With what pallid musings would you replace this vivid testimony? Then let it be; live with it. Say, rather: I really cannot explain why good things happen, things almost too wonderful to be true—but I believe they do. That's what "miracle" means.

The raising of the daughter of Jarius is memorable because it ascribes, for the first time, Jesus' power not only over demons, or disease, but over death itself. Immense emotional distress is followed by "great amazement." It is a little story of death and resurrection. Mark speaks of "fear and trembling"; Soren Kierkegaard, recognizing that this moment lies close to the root of faith, took up the song: "The absurd [signifies] ... the fact that with God all things are possible. The absurd is not one of the factors which can be discriminated within the proper compass of the understanding: it is not identical with the improbable, the unexpected, the unforeseen."[36] Mark says the people were "*seized with great amazement*"; ethics may be concerned primarily with what we do, but religion is primarily concerned with what is done to us, what happens to us—the passive or receptive aspect of power.

The belief that Jesus' crucifixion demonstrates God's power over death, in his own dying and rising to new life, may have been on Mark's mind when he told the story of the young girl who is raised up, again to walk about and to hunger.

Jesus dies and rises again to new life in our hearts and minds, and in our testimonies of word and deed, much as he did for Mark the Evangelist. With this plain-spoken text he plants the seed of faith even today. In this sense— the most important sense—the text of this seminal Gospel is not past tense but entirely present tense. What a blessing it is to be hungry—I mean literally to hunger for food! Hunger is not the same as starvation. Without hunger there would be no tasting the world's smorgasbord of delights. Once again, the reciprocal phrases from the famous prayer of St. Francis, "Lord make me an instrument of thy peace," come to mind: "For it is in giving that we receive, it is in pardoning that we are pardoned, and it is in dying that we are born to eternal life." What we do for others contains what we seek for ourselves; what we do here and now contains what we seek in eternity.

SEVENTEEN

Is not this the carpenter, the son of Mary?

Mark 6:1-13 *And he went out from thence, and came into his own country; and his disciples follow him. And when the Sabbath day was come, he began to teach in the synagogue: and many hearing him were astonished, saying, From whence hath this man these things? And what wisdom is this which is given unto him, that even such mighty works are wrought by his hands? Is not this the carpenter, the son of Mary, the brother of James and Joses [Joseph], and of Juda, and Simon? And are not his sisters here with us? And they were offended at him. But Jesus said unto them, A prophet is not without honor, but in his own country, and among his own kin, and in his own house. And he could there do no mighty work, save that he laid his hands upon a few sick folk, and healed them. And he marveled because of their unbelief. And he went round about the villages, teaching.*

And he called unto him the twelve, and began to send them forth by two and two; and gave them power over unclean spirits; and commanded them that they should take nothing for their journey, save a staff only; no scrip, no bread, no money in their purse; but be shod with sandals; and not put on two coats. And he said unto them, In what place soever ye enter into an house, there abide till ye depart from that place. And whosoever shall not receive you, nor hear you, when ye depart thence, shake off the dust under your feet for a testimony against them. Verily I say unto you, It shall be more tolerable for Sodom and Gomorrha in that day of judgment, than for that city. And they went out, and preached that men should repent. And they cast out many devils, and anointed with oil many that were sick, and healed them.

That there were doubters of this Jesus, and skeptics and scorners—not just among the power elite of church and state but among the common folk— Mark does not deny. An indication of the skepticism is the recognition of his family—his mother Mary and brothers (four are named) and sisters (none are named). The doctrine of "the perpetual virginity of Mary" has some explaining to do. Mark never speaks of Jesus' birth, nor Mary's virginity, unlike Matthew (see 1: 18ff.) and Luke (see 1: 18ff.). Curiously, though, Joseph goes unmentioned in this passage of Mark. Luke's parallel passage (Luke 4: 22), notes Joseph but not the brothers and sisters.

All in all, family problems are a wonderfully humanizing element in the story: "And they made it difficult for him," as Lattimore translates in our vernacular. A famous word, also humanizing, follows: "No prophet is rejected except in his own country, and among his own kinsmen, and in his own house." We are accustomed to the phrase, "is not without honor," where Lattimore bluntly translates, "is rejected."

The power to heal (except for a few minor cases, Mark comments) abandons Jesus, along with the lack of faith among the people in "his own country." This is surprising. Can his power be dependent on their receptivity? I previously noted Plato's idea of power as both the capacity to influence and the capacity to be influenced. The spiritual power that surrounds Jesus seems almost a force-field, something in which either we swim—Plato would have said "participate"—or else are left, like a fish out of water, high and dry.

Here Jesus-the-community-organizer is seen: "And he summoned the twelve and began to send them out two by two." Exorcism of "unclean spirits" is their first-named task; we note that this is not the sole province of Jesus. And they are to take nothing with them that could make them self- sufficient; hence they will depend entirely on the kindness of strangers. Here another famous saying is applied to those who fail the test of kindness and receptivity: "And when a place will not receive you and people will not listen to you, as you leave it shake the dust from the soles of your feet in witness against them." Ouch! This "Eat my dust!" saying reminds us that Jesus did not invariably display a sweet disposition. I conclude, nor need we!

"And they went forth and preached the message of repentance…," sounding the same note that we heard in the first chapter: "Repent, and believe in the Gospel." The Greek word in these places is *metanoia*, meaning change your mind, or turn around entirely, or perhaps "rethink everything!" Our word "repent," while not an inaccurate translation, has taken on moralistic connotations. I have called it "new-mindedness," something we are turning toward as much as, or more than, something we are turning away from.[37]

New-mindedness (*metanoia*) is a key word in the gospel, as are parable, power, demon, faith, and kingdom (*basileia*). Consider rethinking "faith"— faith not as a rule of belief or behavior that excludes other ways of seeing and being, but faith as a dynamic and transforming power, a capacity for new-mindedness, a way of seeing and a way of being that opens new possibilities. I have called attention at various points in this commentary to the way that Jesus appears to be deeply rooted in the traditions of his inherited faith, but also appears to be remarkably free in his handling of tradition. He is a protean figure. This may help explain why Jesus drew many people to him, and why others recoiled from him with hostility. We may see both kinds of people in our personal experience, and we may also recognize from time to time both tendencies in ourselves.

To change your mind is to choose something new and different. James Luther Adams paraphrased Augustine: *Love is an act of will. We choose that which we love.* If so, be mindful in your loving.

EIGHTEEN

Whatsoever thou ask of me, I will give it thee

Mark 6: 14-29 *And king Herod heard of him; (for his name was spread abroad:) and he said, That John the Baptist was risen from dead, and therefore mighty works do show forth themselves in him. Others said, That it is Elias. And others said, That it is a prophet, or as one of the prophets. But when Herod himself had sent forth and laid hold upon John, and bound him in prison for Herodias' sake, his brother Philip's wife: for he had married her. For John has said unto Herod, It is not lawful for thee to have thy brother's wife. Therefore Herodias had a quarrel against him, and would have killed him; but she could not: for Herod feared John, knowing that he was a just man and an holy, and observed him; and when he heard him, he did many things, and heard him gladly. And when a convenient day was come, that Herod on his birthday made a supper to his lords, high captains, and chief estates of Galilee; and when the daughter of the said Herodias came in, and danced., and pleased Herod and them that sat with him, the king said unto the damsel, Ask of me whatsoever thou whilt, and I will give it thee. And he sware unto her, Whatsoever thou shalt ask of me, I will give it thee, unto the half of my kingdom. And she went forth, and said unto her mother, What shall I ask? And she said, The head of John the Baptist. And she came in straightway with haste unto the king, and asked, saying, I will that thou give* *me by and by in a charger the head of John the Baptist. And the king was exceeding sorry; yet for his oath's sake, and for their sakes which sat with him, he would not reject her. And immediately the king sent an executioner, and commanded his head to be brought: and he went and beheaded him in the prison, and brought his head in a charger, and gave it to the damsel: and the damsel gave it to her mother. And when his disciples heard of it, they came and took up his corpse, and laid it in a tomb.*

This violent death is so matter-of-factly told that it takes our breath away.

We want to know: What was Herod thinking? And Herodias? And Salome? But Mark does not say. Homer would have strung out the story for pages, showing us every detail of action and emotion. Mark gives us a few plain-spoken, factual sentences, leaving background emotion and foreground detail for our minds to paint.

Mark notes that various theories of Jesus' identity were circulating: that he is John the Baptist raised from the dead, or the prophet Elijah, who never died, or a "latter-day prophet," one who comes after the recognized "age of the prophets" was closed. In verse 14 we find an astonishing explanation held by some about Jesus' "powers": John's prophetic powers have been transferred and live on in him. The King James Version's, "Therefore mighty works do shew themselves forth in him," sounds grandly archaic, as its translators intended. "For that reason the powers were working in him" (Lattimore) is more expressive of our developing image of the man and his drama. No wonder, then, the prominence of the story of the death of the Baptist in the story of Jesus! It suggests, again, that Jesus' ministry took up when and where John's broke off. Reference to John's burial by "his disciples" is evidence that the Baptist had his own, independent following people who may or may not have attached themselves to Jesus after John's death.

To return to the question that occasioned the story of John the Baptist: Who is this Jesus? Mark's text shows that this question was hotly discussed in Jesus' own time and in the generation following his death, when Mark and the other Gospels were being composed. It is either something he was reticent to reveal, or deliberately hid, or did not himself know. Scholars have said that the Gospels were written to show that Jesus was the Messiah, "the anointed one" appointed by God to deliver the people (setting the stage for endless argument over what those terms mean.) But did Jesus himself have a "Messianic consciousness"? Here scholars disagree over the evidence, which is probably inherently unclear. Usually the Gospels do not discuss subjective thoughts or feelings, but only imply them by outward words and deeds.

Consider the attempt to "explain" Jesus by reference to a traditional role or type or title. (Could *you* be "explained" to others in such a way? Would you object, if they did?) All such explanations must be discounted; they are at best partial truths. The essential truth of a person is always something else, something unique, a new being. No wonder the best of our faith tradition has insisted on the humanity of Jesus. His humanity is the prism through which divinity is refracted.

Mark conveys the sense that, whoever he was, he was an extraordinary man. Not incidentally, Mark also conveys that he was a real human being, not a supernatural or ghostly being, nor an imaginative creation, as some allege. Were he either a mythical or a fictional figure, our view of him would be radically altered. For instance, the Book of Jonah is a short story about a fictional prophet named Jonah, in contrast for example to the prophet Amos, whose book clearly reflects the labors of an historical person. It seems to me equally clear that the Gospels witness to many historical persons, of whom Jesus is one.

Mark's question continues today: What was his extraordinariness? As much as the believers, it bedevils the debunkers, like Hugh Schonfield in *The Passover Plot,* a brilliant attempt to explain everything in this story, as if it were literally true. A similarly misplaced literalism is found, for instance, in the explanation of Moses' parting of the waters of the Red Sea: a strong wind blew the waters aside, or that is was really a shallow "reed sea" in a time of drought, etc. The truth is surely much simpler: an ancient legend which fits a theological theme has been "historicized"—told as if it literally happened—in the rabbinic retellings during several centuries. Nevertheless, there can be no doubt that the ancient Hebrew people escaped from slavery in Egypt.

Herod's answer to the question of Jesus' identity provides a bridge to the tale of the tetrarch, his wife Herodias, her daughter (Salome, the other Gospels tell us), and John the Baptist. This fabulous short story, which Mark imports into the story of Jesus, was set to music by Richard Strauss in the famous opera, "Salome."

The story of the death of John the Baptist is a psychological morality play. Each character plays his or her role, including the prophet, who "speaks truth to power," with dire consequences for himself. He is assassinated as a threat to the ruling Herodian family, much as Jesus will be executed on an unjust charge of sedition. That the story is so fully told by Mark is further evidence of the centrality of the Baptist to the followers of Jesus, and of the transforming effect of his death on Jesus and his community. The wisdom of hindsight also tells us it was a history-changing event for the empire. From this time "the politics of Jesus" begins to transform the politics of the Caesars, even to the present day.[41]

NINETEEN

They were as sheep not having a shepherd

Mark 6: 30-56 *And the apostles gathered themselves together unto Jesus, and told him all things, but what they had done, and what they had taught. And he said unto them, Come ye yourselves apart into a desert place, and rest a while: for there were many coming and going, and they had no leisure so much as to eat. And they departed into a desert place by ship privately. And the people saw them departing, and many knew him, and ran afoot thither out of all cities, and outwent [i.e., went out to] them, and came together unto him. And Jesus, when he came out, saw much people, and was moved with compassion toward them, because they were as sheep not having a shepherd: and he began to teach them many things. And when the day was now far spent, his disciples came unto him, and said, This is a desert place, and now the time is far passed: Send them away, that they may go into the country round about, and into the villages, and buy themselves bread: for they have nothing to eat. He answered and said unto them, Give ye them to eat. And they say unto him, Shall we go and buy two hundred pennyworth of bread, and give them to eat? He saith unto them, How many loaves have ye? go and see. And when they knew, they say, Five, and two fishes. And he commanded them to make all sit down by companies upon the green grass. And they sat down in ranks, by hundreds, and by fifties. And when he had* *taken the five loaves and the two fishes, he looked up to heaven, and blessed, and brake the loaves, and gave them to his disciples to set before them; and the two fishes divided among them all. And they did all eat, and were filled. And they took up twelve baskets full of the fragments, and of the fishes. And they that did eat of the loaves were about five thousand men.*

And straightway he constrained his disciples to get into the ship, and to go to the other side before unto Bethsaida, while he sent away the people. And when he had sent them away, he departed into a mountain to pray. And when even was come, the ship was in the midst of the sea, and he alone on the land.

And he saw them toiling in rowing; for the wind was contrary unto them: and about the fourth watch of the night he cometh unto them, walking upon the sea, and would have passed by them. But when they saw him walking upon the sea, they supposed it had been a spirit, and cried out: For they all saw him, and were troubled. And immediately he talked with them, and saith unto them, Be of good cheer: it is I; be not afraid. And he went up unto them into the ship; and the wind ceased: and they were sore amazed in themselves beyond measure, and wondered. For they considered not the miracle of the loaves: for their heart was hardened. And when they had passed over, they came into the land of Gennesaret, and drew to the shore. And when they were come out of the ship, straightway they knew him, and ran through that whole region round about, and began to carry about in beds those that were sick, where they heard he was. And whithersoever he entered, into villages, or cities, or country, they laid the sick in the streets, and besought him that they might touch if it were but the border of his garment: and as many as touched him were made whole.

The story begins in a remarkably matter-of-fact way. The disciples "report in" and Jesus decided it's time for a little "R and R," or rest, at least. But people scope them out and find them in "a deserted place." They arrive in droves. Again we see Jesus and his disciples beleaguered by crowds of importunate folk. They are not just common folk, or peasantry; they are, as John Dominic Crossan accents, "the destitute poor." Jesus is compassionate: "And he was sorry for them, because they were like sheep without a shepherd," and he began to teach them. The image of this good shepherd as the pastor is a model of ministry as poignant and valid today as then.

Here follows "the feeding of the 5000," the first of several versions of the tale in the synoptic Gospels. (See Matthew 14: 13ff. and Luke 9: 10ff. for parallel versions of "the feeding of the five thousand"; see Matthew 15: 32ff. and Mark 8: 1ff. for parallel versions of "the feeding of the four thousand.") Clearly these feeding stories were popular in the early church. What may have begun in oral tradition as a single story of a miraculous mass feeding had become, by the time of Mark's writing, two distinct events, each with its symbolic meaning.

Again and again we see that "literal" stories are also symbolic stories, or what might better be called parabolic stories. The main numerological clue is the number of baskets left over after the feedings. After the feeding of the 5000, twelve baskets are left, perhaps representing the twelve tribes of Israel. After the feeding of the 4000, seven baskets are left, perhaps representing the seven congregations within the early church. The moral of these twin stories: The abundance Jesus brings suffices for Jews and Gentiles alike.

What can we say? No wonder church picnics, potlucks, and pancake breakfasts are popular events! Church treasurers like the story, too, since the "giving from our abundance" theme nicely trumps our cautious and stingy tendencies: Don't worry that there will not be enough! The Lord will provide! "Self-fulfilling prophesy" is usually applied to negative situations, but here it applies to the positive situation, rather like the now-familiar slogan, "Build it and they will come."

Five loaves and two fish are enough, divided and blessed by Jesus, to feed everyone. They gather, Mark tells, in groups of 50 and 100. Number symbolism again seems to be involved, as the comment indicates: "They had not understood about the loaves, but their hearts had become impenetrable." The supposed lack of comprehension (attributed to a spiritual hard- heartedness) places dimly remembered events in a new light: "We had no idea what this meant at the time, but now we see." We ask: What has changed between *then* and *now*? Is there an analogue to this "revisioning" of reality in our own experience?

When Jesus walks on water, over the stormy sea, the disciples are afraid, and he reassures them that it is he himself, not a phantom or an apparition. When he boards the ship "the wind fell." Again a teaching story: Jesus' simple presence stills the threatening gale.

"Wonders never cease," we like to say. Miracles are just that, wonders. There are scientific explanations of "beautiful" sunsets, but not of the feeling that floods our being in the face of a beautiful sunset, or better yet, a rainbow. The wonder of the rainbow is not just the scientifically describable optical effect of light passing through a rainy sky; it's the fact that we have eyes that take it in and minds that imbue it with affective meaning. This is serious business; it's important that our spirits respond to beauty and not say, "Well, it's *really* just some refracted light." To reduce reality to facts, as determined by objective standards, is called reductionism. Reductive thinking is depressing. It's easy to believe in bad things happening, but can we believe in good things happening? Reductive thinking also falsifies reality; it starves the spirit within. For we do not "live by bread alone but by every word that proceeds out of the mouth of God" (Matthew 4:4) So too our humanity does not live by well-reasoned explanation alone, but by the inclination of our hearts.

In the background of the feeding stories may be the memory of Moses feeding "the children of Israel" in the wilderness for forty years on "manna from heaven," and perhaps also the story of Jesus in the wilderness with the wild beasts for forty days and fed by the angels.

It seems odd that Mark should draw a connection between the disciples' failure to understand about the loaves, and their astonishment that Jesus should walk on water and still the wind. What do you think? I think that Mark is telling us, again and again, that when Jesus was with us, we were clueless about him. Only now that he is gone do we begin to know him. What a paradox!

A mytho-theological observation: To put us to the test, God wants us to know: Do my people use the freedom I've given them for good or for ill? God passes among them in full disguise, to observe without being observed. Only after the fact, when it is too late for us to wise up and adjust our behavior, do we understand. Many stories have employed this device, for instance, Shakespeare in "Measure for Measure," or the familiar children's story, "Stone Soup."

The chapter ends with more and more healings, seemingly scores more, effected by no more than touching "the hem of his mantle." Is this a world even we, in our age of cynicism and fear, might inhabit? What kind of change of heart, what *metanoia*, would that require of us?

TWENTY

Evil things come from within

Mark 7: 1-23 *Then came together unto him the Pharisees, and certain of the scribes, which came from Jerusalem. And when they saw some of his disciples eat bread with defiled, that is to say, with unwashen, hands, they found fault. For the Pharisees and all the Jews, except they wash their hands oft, eat not, holding the tradition of the elders. And when they come from the market, except they wash, they eat not. And many other things there be, which they have received to hold, as the washing of cups, and pots, brazen vessels, and of tables. Then the Pharisees and scribes asked him, Why wash not thy disciples according to the tradition of the elders, but eat bread with unwashen hands? He answered and said unto them, Well hath Esaias [Isaiah] prophesied of you hypocrites, as it is written, This people honoureth me with their lips, but their heart is far from me. Howbeit in vain do they worship me, teaching for doctrines the commandments of men. For laying aside the commandment of God, ye hold the tradition of men, as the washing of pots and cups: and many other such like things ye do. And he said unto them, Full well ye reject the commandment of God, that ye may keep your own tradition. For Moses said, Honour thy father and thy mother; and, Whoso curseth father or mother, let him die the death: But ye say, If a man shall say to his father or mother, It is Corban, that is to say, a gift, by whatsoever thou mightest be profited by me, he shall be free. And ye suffer* *him no more to do ought for his father or his mother: Making the word of God of none effect through your tradition, which ye have delivered: and many such things do ye.*

And when he had called all the people unto him, he said unto them, Hearken unto me every one of you, and understand: There is nothing from without a man, that entering into him can defile him: but the things which come out of him, those are they that defile the man. If any man have ears to hear, let him hear.

And when he was entered into the house from the people, his disciples asked him concerning the parable. And he saith unto them, Are ye so without understanding also? Do ye not perceive, that whatsoever thing from without entereth into the man, it cannot defile him; because it entereth not into his heart, but into the belly, and goeth out into the draught, purging all meats? [Note: the KJV here follows ancient texts that omit Mark's probably interpolated comment: "(Thus he declared all foods clean.)"] And he said, That which cometh out of the man, that defileth the man. For from within, out the heart of men, proceed evil thoughts, adulteries, fornications, murders, thefts, covetousness, wickedness, deceit, lasciviousness, an evil eye, blasphemy, pride, foolishness: All these evil things come from within, and defile the man.

Conflicts with the Pharisees—the strict or legalistic party of the Jewish establishment—arise over the rules of ritual purity, and sometimes hygienic practice, like hand-washing. This section has the feeling of early-Christian conflict with Judaism, when Gentiles were entering the Christian fold. Most of the dialogue on ritual purity and keeping the ancient traditions and religious laws is confusing. Yet one famous simplicity, turning the old rules on their head, stands out: "There is nothing which can go into a man from the outside and defile him; but it is what comes out of a man that defiles him." (Lattimore) We wouldn't want to get overly literal about this, but we get the idea. Mark states it in a form that sets his Christian Judaism at absolute odds with orthodox Judaism: "Thus he made all food clean."

How could so conservative a religion as Christianity was soon to become, come out of such a radical departure from tradition? It's a long and murky story. The question arose, does the gospel "abolish" the Jewish Law (Torah), or does it "fulfill" it? The latter, less radical position, which we see more clearly in Matthew, will soon take ascendancy; in fact Matthew's Jesus, with his "sermon on the mount" (Matthew chapters 5-7) is seen as a new Moses, one who brings commandments that will supplant and succeed, or at least supplement, those of Torah. One verse in that "sermon" states: "Think not that I have come to abolish the law and the prophets; I have come not to abolish them but to fulfill them" (Matthew 5: 17). Lattimore translates, "I have not come to *destroy* them but to *complete* them."

There were early Christian groups, followers of Marcion, who believed that for a Christian the Jewish Law was abolished by the coming of Jesus. Some went so far as to repudiate Hebrew Scripture and even the creator God, Yahweh, the fountainhead of its sacred traditions. After some struggle, the Church rejected this radical Gnostic view. It held that Jesus as the Christ did not destroy, but completed the prophetic-ethical thrust of Judaism, rooted not in an other-worldly spirituality of "knowing" (*gnosis*) but in historical communities of faith. Had this version of Christianity prevailed the loss would have been immense and irreparable. Those who romanticize the Gnostics and their writings as an alternative to what became normative in Christianity should read this as a cautionary tale. James Luther Adams liked to say, "A purely spiritual religion is a purely spurious religion," for it does not deal with the common stuff of life, and it has not undergone its "passage to India"—as in E. M. Forester's tale of propriety overwhelmed by the passions.

Krister Stendahl, one of my teachers of New Testament, spoke of Christians as "honorary Jews." This is the ultimate compliment to Judaism, to recognize that gentiles have taken the Jewish God as their own. It not only puts a nice spin on the many centuries of tangled relations between Christians and Jews; their "way of Jesus" may be different but their God is the same. To speak of the *New* Testament is not to slight the *Old* Testament but to acknowledge dependency on it. There is much evidence in the Gospels that Jesus understood himself and remained to the end a faithful Jew.

How difficult it is to have faith, these days! I am reminded of Gerhardt Ebeling's sly assertion: "The purpose of theology is to make preaching as hard for the preacher as it has to be."[39] More simply stated, if a theology is simple it is probably simplistic, a falsification of the truth. "When I was a child I thought as a child… but when I became a man I put away childish things"—famous phrases from Paul's "hymn to love" (1 Corinthians 13). This, I think, is our universal human experience: We "succeed" ourselves in the process of growing up; but a morally mature "growing up" affirms and incorporates the self that we have known from the start of life. It is good to be rooted in a child-like faith, if in adulthood you have managed to transform that faith, finding even your "second naïveté."

Creative choices in life always depend on the exercise of thoughtful judgment, taking all sides of a question into account. Fundamentalism is fatally marked by its impatience with ambiguity and uncertainty. A sense of humor loves ambiguity, paradox, and irony: *ambiguity*, not to be confused with fuzzy thinking; *paradox*, not to be confused with self-contradiction; and *irony*, not to be confused with sarcasm.

The issue, here—why is "truth" so difficult to get at, leaving us vulnerable to so many hucksters?—is at root metaphysical. I'll put it this way: The material world is dense, almost impenetrable. It defiles the sacred, it drowns the spirit, and it deafens us with its cacophonous noise. Almost, but not utterly. I saw an iris breaking through the asphalt at the edge of my driveway the other day—a veritable miracle and a nice little parable of the Spirit that is Holy.

TWENTY-ONE

He maketh both the deaf to hear and the dumb to speak

Mark 7:24-37 *And from thence he arose, and went into the borders of Tyre and Sidon, and entered into an house, and would have no man know it: but he could not be hid. For a certain woman, whose young daughter had an unclean spirit, heard of him, and came and fell at his feet: The woman was a Greek, a Syro-Phoenician by nation; and she besought him that he would cast forth the devil out of her daughter. But Jesus said unto her, Let the children first be filled: for it is not meet to take the children's bread, and to cast it unto the dogs. And she answered and said unto him, Yes, Lord: yet the dogs under the table eat of the children's crumbs. And he said unto her, for this saying go thy way; the devil is gone out of thy daughter. And when she was come to her house, she found the devil gone out, and her daughter laid upon the bed.*

And again, departing from the coasts of Tyre and Sidon, he came unto the sea of Galilee, through the midst of the coasts of Decapolis. And they bring unto him one that was deaf, and had an impediment in his speech; and they beseech him to put his hand upon him. And he took him aside from the multitude, and put his fingers into his ears, and he spit, and touched his tongue; and looking up to heaven, he sighed, and saith unto him, EPHPHATHA, that is,

> *Be opened. And straightway his ears were opened, and the string of his tongue was loosed, and he spake plain. And he charged them that they should tell no man: but the more he charged them, so much the more a great deal they published it; and were beyond measure astonished, saying, He hath done all things well: he maketh both the deaf to hear, and the dumb to speak.*

Two stories follow. The first is of the Phoenician woman from Syria, a gentile; this is another instance of a woman taking an important role in Mark's Gospel. Her ironic plea, "Even the dogs under the table eat of the children's crumbs," is a parable: Even the gentiles whom you disdain seek the meager scraps of your healing power. It seems unlikely that such a rebuke would have been remembered and recorded if an actual event did not occasion it. If so, the story reflects a surprisingly prejudiced and callous attitude on the part of Jesus toward gentiles, for he will not help the woman and her young daughter, one who is "possessed by an unclean spirit." He speaks metaphorically of the Jews as the children and gentiles as dogs, saying, in response to the woman's appeal for an exorcism for her daughter: "the children"—the rightful heirs—go before "the dogs"—the gentiles! The Phoenician woman, uniquely in the Gospels, answers him as he has been answering his own detractors, with a well-sharpened wit. Neither does Jesus take offense at her response but validates it: "Because of this saying, go! The demon has left your daughter." Curiously, it's almost as if *her words* were powerful enough to effect the exorcism, and Jesus merely confirms it. Did this encounter so quickly cause him to change his mind about gentiles—as if the imperative of *metanoia*, "newmindedness," applied also to himself? There is something about importunate behavior itself, such as this woman displays, that the gospel commends.

The incident reminds us of what is apparent on close reading of Mark, that Jesus was a Jew who seems not to have ventured into gentile territory or towns, and to have avoided gentile contact entirely. He apparently thought of gentiles as outside his mission. And yet, confronted with a gentile woman who sees miraculous powers working in him, he seems forced to broaden his outlook! We might say that Jesus did not entirely appreciate the universality of his mission and message until he was taught by this gentile woman. That would seem an odd conclusion, on any orthodox assumptions about Jesus' supposed divine omniscience. But why else would Mark tell the story in this way?

Another story of healing follows about a man who was deaf and almost without speech. The method of curing him seems primitive, with fingers in his ears and spit on his tongue, and a groaning noise while looking up to the sky and uttering one word, *Ephphatha*, which Mark translates, "Be opened." The preservation of this Aramaic word may indicate that the story is early and authentic, and the word a magical incantation. Probably the narrative line on which these episodes are hung is not historical. Mark seems to have been a collector of traditions, reporting stories as they were passed down, and fitting them into his narrative.

Giving sight to the blind and hearing to the deaf are not simply miracles of healing for individuals; they are signs of transformation wrought by the coming of the Messiah, the one given to rule in the kingdom of God. I have always found the imagery of Isaiah's messianic prophesies profoundly moving—the Messiah as "servant-leader," the world as a great tent, the universal justice to which the people of God are called, the parent-like care they have received from God. Ponder these lines from the Book of Isaiah, chapter 42 (Revised Standard Version):

> Behold my servant, whom I uphold,
>   my chosen, in whom my soul delights;
> I have put my Spirit upon him,
>   he will bring forth justice to the nations… .
> Thus says God, the LORD [Yahweh],
>   who created the heavens and stretched them out,
>   who spread forth the earth and what comes from it,
>   who gives breath to the people upon it
>   and spirit to those who walk in it:
> "I am the LORD, I have called you in righteousness,
>   I have taken you by the hand and kept you;
> I have given you as a covenant to the people,
>   a light to the nations,
>   to open the eyes that are blind,

> To bring out the prisoners from the dungeon,
>   from the prison those who sit in darkness....
> Behold the former things have come to pass,
>   and new things I now declare;
> Before they spring forth
>   i tell you of them.

How then does the Messiah come, but by our own fulfillment of the covenant appointed to us by the Creator, the one who "stretches out the heavens" to give us an earthly place in which to be and to thrive? James Luther Adams took a political concept, *covenant,* and made it into an ontological concept, *being,* when he spoke of "the covenant of being," a perception of reality as "gift and task." The covenant to which Isaiah calls the people is both a sacred gift, a "light to the nations," and a moral task, "to bring out the prisoners from the dungeon."

Though prophesied, Mark is telling us, the messianic age remains for the time being hidden: hence the command of silence, to keep the messianic secret entirely secret. Yet the secret is being revealed again and again in the mighty works of Jesus, for "he makes the deaf hear and the speechless speak." These are the signs of the coming of Messiah, the anointed one, named by the prophet Isaiah. The coming kingdom of God is a moving train and many are climbing on board. An intangible sense of momentum is building.

What is the moral legacy of such stories? Compassion for those who suffer from any oppression. To suffer means to be subject to something beyond our control, such as sickness, or want, or insanity, or incarceration—conditions we often shun, as when we are indifferent to the sufferer. Mark's few words are charged with feeling: "They *beseech* him to put his hand upon him"—or again, "a certain woman... came and *fell at his feet.*" So few words, such profound expressions of human longing to be whole!

There may be times when we feel we can only say, "I've been abandoned" or, perhaps, "I've been betrayed." Jesus himself seems to come to the edge of such times again and again—one of the reasons why the Gospels are so moving.

The deepest questions of faith do not arise when our lives are "just fine," but when we meet difficulty and loss. In my book *If Yes Is the*

Answer, What Is the Question? I framed this question, *Is help available when I need it?* It is the kind of personal question that no one can answer for us, but our ability to answer *Yes* is a starting point for an authentic sense of faith—faith as confidence and trust, inward qualities of heart and mind that transcend every circumstance.[40] Is help available when I need it? Can I answer, *yes?* Of course, those who profess never to need help, who are quite certain they never will need help, whose total reliance is summed up by an Emersonian self-reliance, may brush this question aside. How lonely they must be!

TWENTY-TWO
Why does this generation seek after a sign?

Mark 8: 1-26 *In those days the multitude being very great, and having nothing to eat, Jesus called his disciples unto him, and saith unto them, I have compassion on the multitude, because they have now been with me three days, and have nothing to eat: and if I send them away fasting to their own houses, they will faint by the way: for divers of them came from far. And his disciples answered him, From whence can a man satisfy these men with bread here in the wilderness? And he asked them, How many loaves have ye? And they said, Seven. And he commanded the people to sit down on the ground: and he took the seven loaves, and gave thanks, and brake, and gave to his disciples to set before them; and they did set them before the people. And they had a few small fishes: and he blessed, and commanded to set them also before them. So they did eat, and where filled: and they took up of the broken meat that was left seven baskets. And they that had eaten were about four thousand: and he sent them away.*

And straightway he entered into a ship with his disciples, and came into the parts of Dalmanutha. And the Pharisees came forth, and began to question with him, seeking of him a sign from heaven, tempting him. And he sighed deeply in his spirit, and saith, Why doth this generation seek after a sign? Verily I say unto you, There shall be no sign given unto this generation. And he left them, and entering into the ship again departed to the other side.

Now the disciples had forgotten to take bread, neither had they in the ship with them more than one loaf. And he charged them, saying, Take heed, beware of the leaven of the Pharisees, and of the leaven of Herod. And they reasoned among themselves, saying, It is because we have no bread. And when Jesus knew it, he saith unto them, Why reason ye, because ye have no bread? Perceive ye not yet, neither understand? Have ye your heart yet hardened? Having eyes, see ye not? And having ears, hear ye not? And do ye not remember? When I brake the five loaves among five thousand, how many baskets full of fragments took ye up? And they said, Seven. And he said unto them, How is it that ye do not understand?

And he cometh to Bethsaida; and they bring a blind man unto him, and besought him to touch him. And he took the blind man by the hand, and led him out of the town; and when he had spit on his eyes, and put his hands upon him, he asked him if he saw ought. And he looked up, and said, I see men as trees, walking. After that he put his hands again upon his eyes, and made him look up: and he was restored, and saw every man clearly. And he sent him away to his house, saying, Neither go into the town, nor tell it to any in the town.

Commentators call the story of the feeding of the four thousand a doublet, since it is so similar to the feeding of the 5000, shortly before. So are we to suppose that Jesus did the same compassionate act twice, or that one historical event has wended its way through two oral traditions, both coming down to Mark, who preserves both? Here is the dilemma of interpretation: Are we after the ever-elusive, perpetually debated "historical Jesus," or are we seeking to understand this text, this Gospel which has done its seminal work since the time of its composition?

If the latter, then we will note the number-symbolism involved in these two feeding stories; indeed, Mark calls attention to it when Jesus berates the disciples for their incomprehension. Twelve baskets of crumbs gathered from the five loaves stand for the Jews, with their twelve tribes and five books of Moses. Seven baskets of crumbs gathered from seven loaves, plus "a few fish," may signify the seventy Gentile nations.

Maybe. The question, "How shall we have enough bread in the desert to be able to feed these people?" may indicate that these miraculous feedings recall the manna with which God fed the Israelites during their wilderness wanderings: Jesus is a new Moses.

Another interpretation: the story prefigures the Christian Eucharist (Communion, Last Supper commemoration); Mark gives no hint of this, but the story feeds this symbolic understanding.

Mark seems to understand this feeding of the 4000 as a sign of Jesus' messianic mission, for he follows the story with the Pharisees' demand for "a sign from the sky," and another instance of the disciples' faithless anxiety, when they cross to the other side of the lake and worry over having only one loaf of bread. Now Jesus really unloads on this weak-kneed and this utterly obtuse band of disciples. He asks them to read the number symbolism.

"Why does this generation seek a sign? Truly I tell you, no sign shall be given to this generation." Matthew adds an exception to Mark's "no sign" stricture: "except the sign of Jonah," which may signify the Resurrection, since Jonah was resurrected, or at least regurgitated, from the belly of a whale, or at least a large fish. The demand for a "sign," that is, for some display of supernatural power, here as elsewhere comes from adversaries, notably from the Pharisees who want to "test" him. But he refuses; he will wait for God to reveal whatever God will in God's own good time. He will not cross the line between the prophet and the magician.

It seems odd, though, that Mark's "no sign" stricture should follow directly after what seems to be "a sign from heaven" on a grand scale, the feeding story. And that Jesus should complain of his disciples' inability to comprehend its meaning; as if to say, You were given a sign and still you don't understand!

If there are "no signs," no miraculous indicators which put the stamp on Jesus' mission as God's own mission, then the world remains, for the time being, entirely opaque—flesh that is impervious to spirit, darkness that swallows light itself. Religion has always turned on the question of revelation: how do the gods disclose themselves to us? Robert Frost's poem, "Revelation," uses the image of the child's game of Hide and Seek as a metaphor for the self-disclosure, or revelation, of God: "So all who hide too well away / Must speak and tell us where they are."[41]

Rationalists have derided the theological idea of revelation, of God's self- disclosure. Unlike the poets—Dante, Frost, Auden, Dickinson, Eliot, Nemerov—they do not reckon with the passions of our human relationship to transcendence. Howard Nemerov said: "The poet's business is to name as accurately as possible a situation, but a situation which he himself is in. The name he gives ought to be as close a fit with the actuality it summons into being that there remains no room between inside and outside; the thought must be 'like a beast moving in its skin' (Dante)."[42] Would you describe love as a biologist does, or as a lover does? If the latter, you'd not looking at it from the outside, as rationalists want us to do, but from the inside.

Was Mark musing, much as I am? Is this why he goes on to tell the story of the blind man who saw wavering images—"men as trees, walking"—until Jesus with spittle wiped his eyes clean, restoring unclouded vision to him? Howard Nemerov several times uses the image of running water, for instance, "the stillness in moving things," in the great poem "Runes," or tears, in lines which introduce his essay, "On Going Down in History":

> That there should be much goodness in the world,
> Much kindness and intelligence, candor and charm,
> And that it all goes down in the dust after a while:
> This is a subject for the steadiest meditations
> Of the heart and mind, as for the tears
> That clarify the eye toward charity.[43]

Revelation is not simply a matter of seeing what had been obscure; it is seeing with the eyes of love, not something we accomplish on our own, but a gift.

TWENTY-THREE

But whom say ye that I am?

Mark 8: 27 - 9: 1 *And Jesus went out, and his disciples, into the towns of Caesarea Philippi: and by the way he asked his disciples, saying unto them, Whom do men say that I am? And they answered, John the Baptist: but some say, Elias; and others, One of the prophets. And he saith unto them, But whom say ye that I am? And Peter answereth and saith unto him, Thou art the Christ. And he charged them that they should tell no man of him. And he began to teach them, that the Son of man must suffer many things and be rejected of the elders, and of the chief priests, and scribes, and be killed, and after three days rise again. And he spake that saying openly. And Peter took him, and began to rebuke him. But when he had turned about and looked on his disciples, he rebuked Peter, saying, Get thee behind me, Satan: for thou savourest not the things that be of God, but the things that be of men.*

And when he had called the people unto him with his disciples also, he said unto them, Whosoever will come after me, let him deny himself, and take up his cross, and follow me. For whosoever will save his life shall lose it: he whosoever shall lose his life for my sake and the gospel's, the same shall save it. For what shall it profit a man, if he shall gain the whole world, and lose his own soul? Or what shall a man give in exchange for his soul?

Whosoever therefore shall be ashamed of me and of my words in this adulterous and sinful generation; of him also shall the Son of man be ashamed, when he cometh in the glory of his Father with the holy angels. And he said unto them, Verily I say unto you, That there be some of them that stand here, which shall not taste of death, till they have seen the kingdom of God come with power.

"Who do people say that I am?" (Lattimore translation) Jesus' question, the question of his identity, is prophetic. Christians have been asking it and fighting over the answer to it ever since. How we answer this question will tell what we believe the gospel is, what it meant not just to Mark and those who heard his seminal message, but to us today. Jesus' question goes to the heart of the matter.

Three answers are proposed. It is the same question that weighed on Herod's mind (Mark 6: 12 ff.), and similar answers are proposed. He could be John the Baptist raised from the dead. Or he could be Elijah the prophet who was bodily raised in a chariot of fire (Kings 2: 11-12) and is expected to return, or he could simply be "a latter-day prophet"—unusual in that Judaism held that "the age of the prophets" was past. The question remains unanswered; whoever he is, he represents something more than himself alone.

It should be noted that Mark, like the other Gospels, raises not a historical question but a theological question, not a question of fact but a question of faith. Still, theology depends on history insofar as it is an interpretation of history, and therefore is responsible in fundamental ways to historical truth. The Gospel of Mark is not an objective history, and not a biography of Jesus. But if it were purely fictional, as some have argued it is, it would be invalidated as a source of faith. Christian faith and theological reflection on that faith—for instance, making it relevant to contemporary thought—turns on the interpretation of Jesus as "the Christ."

What, then, does "Christ" mean in contemporary terms? A recent answer to this question is offered by Dorothea Solle, in *Christ the Representative*. She sees Jesus as the Christ in that he represents (re-presents, steps in the place of) God's word and will, giving them human form and action. Christians, she says, are similarly called to re-present Jesus' word and will—his message and healing work—ever after.⁴⁴ Thus there is no question that he was a human being, a man who lived at a certain time and a certain place. It is the meaning we draw from his story that makes him the Christ, the representative of God who forms the basic pattern for representations of God's word and will in all succeeding generations, even our own.

Imagine a group of friends asking each other, "Who do you say that I am?" It's an unlikely scene, but suppose we did. We would probably come up with better answers about *others* than we could give about *ourselves*. Albert Camus, the French novelist, once said that no one can say who he or she is, but others must tell us. Strange as it seems, we are largely hidden from ourselves—or, perhaps, we see ourselves in a distorting mirror. This is not what we expect of strong, "self-possessed" people. All of us ask this question; we want to know how others see us. Does this mean that we lack confidence at the core of our being about ourselves? No. Even Jesus, who always seems to speak and act with independence and complete confidence, asks this question. So we are in good company. Our identity is always chosen and created by ourselves, and yet *who we are* depends also on the confirmation of others. We are inextricably social beings, even if we think of ourselves as outsiders or individualists.

Jesus goes on to ask them, But who do *you* say that I am? "Peter answered and said to him, 'You are the Christ.'" The Greek word *Christos* translates the Hebrew word, *Messiah*, which means "the anointed one" of God. For thousands of years kings have been anointed with oil as a sign of their divine right. The Messiah, in ancient Jewish belief, would be a new king, coming by divine power and divine right to rule. It is understandable that the yearning for a king and a kingdom, one like King David's, grew among the Jewish people after the destruction of the ancient kingdoms of Israel and Judah. This yearning reshaped the ancient Jewish faith.

Did Jesus think he was the Messiah? Certainly Mark believes he is the Messiah—albeit in a radically different sense than a worldly ruler—and writes his gospel to show what this means. But the Gospels do not give us access to Jesus' mind, except as it is reflected in his words and deeds. Only once in Mark does he directly assent to

Messianic identity (discussed in chapter 19); here he does not deny it, but commands silence about it.

The central question remains: What does it mean to be "the anointed one"? If Jesus is not defined by ancient traditions or models, how is he defined? He is something like the great king and poet, David; and something like the liberator and law-giver, Moses; and something like the prototypical and ecstatic prophet, Elijah; and even something like the first man, Adam—St. Paul calls him "the second Adam," the one in whose image we are renewed. But he is not simply any of these. Yet another candidate for his identity is especially important in the formation of "the passion narrative" in the Gospels, "the suffering servant," which comes from the book of Isaiah (see Isa. 53). Or is "the suffering servant" not an individual, as interpreters of Isaiah have suggested, but the nation itself, the whole people of God?

Perhaps the most obvious title is *servant*, one who ministers to the needs of others; hence his job description, to teach, to heal, and to organize. Where there are many models, there can be no single or dogmatic truth.

Here again we meet what I think is key to a valid understanding of fundamental religious ideas, such as *God, kingdom of God, and miracle:* They are embedded in mystery. In consequence, when we talk about them we must start from the supposition that we do not entirely know what we are talking about. Now we are ready for the existential question, on which religious meaning always turns: What in this story speaks to me, liberates me, heals me, lifts me up? An endless set of creative possibilities arise from this vantage-point.

The gospel story draws us in, so that its story tends to become our personal story; it is we who are being asked, "But who do you say that I am?"

"Then he warned them to tell no one about him." The previously remarked hidden meaning of his parables and healings now becomes the "Messianic secret." Why the secrecy? It's a puzzle: *what's true is not known, and what's known is not true.* Perhaps the puzzle is solved by adding "not yet." What's true is *not yet known*, and what's known is *not yet true*, for truth is an event *to be known* in the fullness of time.

Is it secret because it depends not on some public, factual knowledge, but on our own personal affirmation? If he is the Christ *to me*, then he is the Christ. And you stand in the same relation to truth. You will answer for yourself, freely, who you believe he is. Coercion contradicts love itself.

Here we have Jesus' first foretelling of his crucifixion and Resurrection. And this same lead disciple, Peter, seeks to contradict him, as if to say: "Oh, that can never happen!" This leads to Jesus' famous rebuke: "Get thee behind me, Satan!" This may seem astonishingly harsh, if we think of Satan as pure evil; but the Biblical Satan functions as "the tempter," the one who puts us to the test by inviting *us* to do evil. Jesus does not directly foretell this of himself, but of "the Son of man" who "must suffer and be rejected by the elders and the high priests, and the scribes, and be killed, and rise up after three days." We assume, and perhaps Mark does also, that Jesus is speaking of himself; and yet the oblique, third person reference to "the Son of man" may mean that he will take on the role or *persona* of this mysterious, heaven-sent figure. He will represent him. The term "Son of man" first appears in the apocalyptic book of Daniel:

> I saw in the night visions,
> And behold, with the clouds of heaven
> There came one like a son of man,
> And he came to the Ancient of Days,
> And was presented before him.
> (Daniel 7: 13)

Peter does not want to hear about crucifixion because he does not want to count the cost. But let's admit it, who does? Again, the gospel causes us to interrogate ourselves.

What follows, in Mark 8: 34 to 9: 1, is the first time Jesus addresses "the multitude together with his disciples," speaking now openly about what Dietrich Bonhoeffer, the German pastor and theologian who was executed for taking part in a plot on Hitler's life, called *the cost of discipleship*: "Take up your cross and follow me. If you wish to save your life you will lose it, and if you lose it for my sake and the gospel's, you will gain it." Many famous and unforgettable phrases crowd this paragraph, which concludes with words of warning for those who are "ashamed of me and my words in this adulterous and sinful generation."

What a powerful emotion is shame! It is probably the best antidote to nicotine addiction: "I was ashamed to be seen smoking, so I quit!" Which is why, if your social group smokes, you smoke: no shame. But Jesus' point is quite the opposite, here. If your social group frowns on the kind of faith he gives us occasion to affirm, and you let that concern for the world's opinion shame you, then you'll never find the kind of faith that cries out, "I believe, help my unbelief!" Talk about tough love!

The formulation, "for my sake and the gospel's," is curious, especially when we see that the parallel passages in Matthew (16: 26) and Luke (9: 24) omit "and the gospel's." Mark may reflect a stage of early Christian thought when "Jesus" and "the gospel," though previously distinct, were now beginning to coalesce. Matthew and Luke abolish any distinction, making "and the gospel's" superfluous. We may ask: does Jesus bring "the gospel," that is, the kingdom of God, or does "the gospel" bring Jesus? That is, do we see the presence and power of "God-ruling" as something that Jesus points to and calls his followers to see and affirm? Or is it that Jesus himself brings the power and presence of God-ruling into the world, as the Christology of the Gospel of John seems to affirm? I would keep them as distinct understandings; there is room and even need, after all, for more than one revelation of the sacred.[45]

The turning point in Mark's Gospel is the turning point in the gospel itself, for here we are told that whatever worldly expectations you had, whatever wishes for your own reward or your own glory you had, forget it. Turn about, repent, think again, be new-minded. Be ready to sacrifice your wealth, your pride, even your life. These words of Jesus address us personally, straight across the centuries, needing not a sentence of scholarly interpretation. They ask for a decision, knowing that everything flows from and depends upon an "original decision," a decision that comes before and impels other decisions. The gospel presses upon us this existential moment. That is not so much what it is *about* as what it *is*.

The flipside of pride is shame, and only faith overcomes both our pride and our shame. They are intimately related. If you have been shamed, you know what injured pride is and that it remains with you for a long time. But Jesus' final word, in this astonishing discourse, is that there will be a final reckoning. Your shame, then, is not your defeat.

TWENTY-FOUR
And he was transfigured before them

Mark 9: 2-10 *And after six days Jesus taketh with him Peter, and James, and John, and leadeth them up into a high mountain apart by themselves: and he was transfigured before them. And his raiment became shining, exceeding white as snow; so as no fuller on earth can white them. And there appeared unto them Elias with Moses: and they were talking with Jesus. And Peter answered and said to Jesus, Master, it is good for us to be here: and let us make three tabernacles; one for thee, and one for Moses, and one for Elias. For he wist [knew] not what to say; for they were sore afraid. And there was a cloud that overshadowed them: and a voice came out of the cloud, saying, This is my beloved Son: hear him. And suddenly, when they had looked round about, they saw no man any more, save Jesus only with themselves. And as they came down from the mountain, he charged them that they should tell no man what things they had seen, till the Son of man were risen from the dead. And they kept that saying with themselves, questioning one with another what the rising from the dead should mean.*

Is the coming of the kingdom of God a sudden, great event that is immanent "before some of those who stand here… taste death"? We want to ask: Maybe so, Jesus, but how will we recognize it? What is this kingdom?

People often assume that the kingdom of God will come as a kind of cataclysm, a sudden event bringing violent destruction upon the world. They think it will be like the flood that, in Noah's time, destroyed the wicked world, with only the deserving few surviving. They usually also assume that they will be among the deserving few!

But perhaps it is not like this at all. Perhaps the kingdom of God is not a destroying but a transforming event, not a once-happening future event but an already-present, spiritual reality, something that changes us from within. Jesus' ability to exorcise demons and cure grave illnesses, Mark shows, is due to a faith so complete that it gives him access to God's ruling power, something already present, available to be grasped. This kingdom of God is always "at hand."

When we hear "kingdom of God" we tend to think of a bounded territory. As previously noted, the Greek phrase, *basileia tou theou*, would be more accurately translated "reign of God," "rule of God," or "God-ruling." By whatever label we should understand this "kingdom" as an active and powerfully transforming spiritual reality, not a piece of heavenly or earthly geography. This kingdom is always present, in faith available to us; but it always transcends this time and place, "out of reach," and therefore never completely realized.

In the story of "the transfiguration" Jesus takes Peter, James, and John—his chief disciples—up on a mountain. There Jesus undergoes a fantastic change: his garments emit a brilliant white light and he meets apparitions of Elijah and Moses, with whom he talks. Why Moses and Elijah? He is like Moses, the deliverer and law-giver of the Israelites, and he is like Elijah, the prophet who defied King Ahab and Queen Jezebel and defeated the prophets of Baal, the chief Canaanite god.

The moral of the story? Jesus is in very good company! The voice from the cloud says of him: "This is my son whom I love; listen to him." The words reaffirm the words heard at Jesus' baptism; it is also possible that the story of the transfiguration came first, in the oral tradition, and that it shaped the story of the baptism.

The sudden disappearance of Moses and Elijah indicates that Mark understands that this was a spiritual apparition, not a physical reality. A divine message is being conveyed, but to Jesus' most trusted companions only. The "secret" has been opened, but not to the public or even the other followers. They are to "tell no one" what they have seen "until the Son of man should rise from the dead." We are told that "they kept his commandment" to keep silence, while wondering what he meant about the Son of man rising from the dead. Here again we meet the messianic secret.

Contemporary Biblical scholars largely agree that Jesus did not himself claim to be the Messiah. This is why our earliest source, Mark, represents his heaven-sent status as Messiah or Son of man as veiled in secrecy. The "messianic secret" explains why, as Mark tells us again and again, even though he was indeed the Messiah at least from the time of his baptism, nobody knew it during his lifetime. They concluded that only after his death on the cross; and they symbolized that belief in the story of the empty tomb and the Resurrection.

This is not said, as some may feel, to demote Jesus' status. It is meant to help us understand the gospel by way of a critical and creative reading of the redemptive message, conveyed by the Gospel of Mark. Mark must have asked himself: Why during Jesus' lifetime was his divine mission not known? His answer was that it was a secret, and it had to remain a secret lest the demonic forces of the world destroy his mission before it could get started. This idea is reflected in the nativity story told by Matthew, where King Herod inquires of the magi when and where the Christ-child—the new king—is to be born, so he can kill him; the "flight into Egypt" by the Holy Family foils Herod the Great's plot. (They were magi—that is, magicians, not kings. What's more, Matthew does not say there were precisely three of them!) We are told that Herod proceeded to have all boys under age two in the region slaughtered—itself a fantastically demonic act and probably apocryphal. Our sense of the fate of Jesus' goodness in a world dominated by evil power is dramatized by Matthew's story.

To my mind what is important is not precisely what happened 2000 years ago, but the spiritual reality—the meaning-giving and motivating elements of consciousness—we live with in the present. I call the primary spiritual reality "the presence of transcendence." Paul Tillich sought to refresh our religious understanding by speaking of "transcendence" not as *above* us, or "heavenly", but as "the depth dimension of existence." He spoke of God as "the ground of being," that which *underlies* existence itself. My colleague David B. Parke writes: "By theology I mean life in depth. Theology invites us into the depths of whatever question, task, or relationship we are involved in. Without depth, or at least openness to depth, there is no theological engagement or promise. In the depths, conversely, everything is theological."[46]

Frank Kermode's *The Genesis of Secrecy* deals with various narratives, but takes the Gospel of Mark as his poster child.[47] In Mark's narrative the central figure is himself a teller of parables that are often obscure. At one point Jesus says, "Nothing is hidden that will not be revealed." Kermode argues that effective stories are always obscure, always lead us to ask "who done it?" or "what does it mean?" or "how will it end?" Nobody wants to read a murder mystery where we find out who the murderer is on page one. Good stories are obscure because the meaning of life, our own life above all, is obscure. Good stories are "true to life" not by being "realistic" but by revealing us to ourselves. Fables, parables, myths, science fiction, operas—these are not realistic, but they are true to life if they reveal some hidden truth about us, and move us to smile or weep.

Every human life is a narrative. Its meaning is not something that we make for ourselves, but something we discover through persistent and hopeful engagement with life. I cannot prove that this is so. It is a statement of faith, something I affirm because it helps me make sense out of life. This is what Mark's Gospel is all about: discovering the way in which transcendence is present—not *was* but *is* present, as much today as ever.

TWENTY-FIVE
Lord, I believe, help thou mine unbelief

Mark 9: 11-29 *And they asked him, saying, why say the scribes that Elias must come first? And he answered and told them, Elias verily cometh first, and restoreth all things; and how it is written that the Son of man, that he must suffer many things, and be set at naught. But I say unto you, that Elias is indeed come, and they have done unto him whatsoever they listed, as it is written of him.*

And when he came to his disciples, he saw a great multitude about them, and the scribes questioning with them. And straightway all the people, when they beheld him, were greatly amazed, and running to him saluted him. And he asked the scribes, what question ye with them? And one of the multitude answered and said, Master, I have brought unto thee my son, which hath a dumb spirit; and wheresoever he taketh him, he teareth him: and he foameth, and gnasheth with his teeth, and pineth away: and I spake to thy disciples that they should cast him out; and they could not. He answereth him, and saith, O faithless generation, how long shall I be with you? How long shall I suffer you? Bring him unto me. And they brought him unto him: and when he saw him, straightway the spirit tare him; and he fell on the ground, and wallowed foaming. And he asked his father, How long is it ago since this came unto him? And he said, Of a child. And ofttimes it hath cast him into the fire, and into the waters, to destroy him: but if thou canst do any thing, have compassion on us, and help us. Jesus said unto him, If thou canst believe, all things are possible to him that believeth. And straightway the father of the child cried out, and said with tears, Lord, I believe; help thou mine unbelief. When Jesus saw that the people came running together, he rebuked the foul spirit, saying unto him, Thou dumb and deaf spirit, I charge thee, come out of him, and enter no more into him. And the spirit cried, and rent him sore, and came out of him: and he was as one dead; insomuch that many said, He is dead. But Jesus took him by the hand, and lifted him up; and he arose. And when he was come into the house, his disciples asked him privately, Why could not we cast him out? And he said unto the, This kind can come forth by nothing, but by prayer and fasting.

In Mark's account Jesus accepts the understanding that John the Baptist was Elijah, returned as precursor to the Son of man, and that the Son of man "must suffer many things." Is he the Son of man, or does he only re-present this heaven-sent figure in human form? Is he telling the story, or living the story, or somehow both—in Mark's mind if not in his own? The Gospel of Mark is the story of a parable-teller whose very life is a parable, a story that may be a tough nut. But when you manage to crack it open, it gives you something nourishing.

The story of the man who brings his demon-possessed son to Jesus directly follows. The father pleads for help from Jesus, because his disciples were not able to. It is a very difficult case, but "if you can," he says, please help. To which Jesus replies: "If you can? All things are possible to him who believes." That is when the father says that "belief," for him, is a constant struggle with "unbelief."

Perhaps faith is what lies along the boundary between unbelief and belief, and is finally the courage to cross over.

Jesus does not say to the man for whom believing is a struggle, "Well, that's not good enough." He knows that when we most need it, when despair beckons, believing never comes easy. Faith that is facile is a fake. He simply goes ahead and commands the evil spirit to come out of the child. And it does come out, literally kicking and screaming. How wonderfully graphic Mark is! The end of the story sustains the mysterious undertone. The disciples— surely, they think, we are among the believers—ask: How come we couldn't do it ourselves? Jesus' reply adds a new twist to what we've heard before: "This kind cannot be made to go forth except by prayer." (Some ancient texts and modern translations such as Lattimore's omit the words "and fasting" after "prayer"; it is probably a late add-on; the essential meaning is not altered: faith-healing is not automatic or magical.) Prayer—not pro-forma prayer, but deeply felt prayer—always involves a struggle of faith, an "I believe, help thou my unbelief," or "let this cup pass from me," or when-all- is-said-and-done "thy will be done."

The prayer of the prosperous may not get beyond giving thanks for, well, prosperity. George Bernard Shaw's character, Lina, says, "The poor do not pray, they beg." We are not, I pray, too proud to beg. But we also know that to pray is finally to surrender our wishes to the will of God. "Thy will be done." Only in God are the wish and the power to accomplish the wish always at one. This is why we do not predict important things, as if we could see the future, but add to our wish, "God willing!"

Do we find ourselves in this story? I find myself in the father of the paralytic boy who cries out, "I believe, help thou my unbelief!" Which is to say, I find in myself a faith that is never a secure possession, never a pat answer, never a "it goes without saying." It is always something I must struggle with and pray that the prayer itself breaks through the surfaces— whether they be slick and shimmering or rough and tough—that we like to keep between ourselves and life itself. "I like a look of agony," said Emily Dickinson; it breaks through complacency and it does not lie.

TWENTY-SIX
If any man desire to be first

Mark 9: 30-50 *And they departed thence, and passed through Galilee; and he would not that any man should know it. For he taught his disciples, and said unto them, The son of man is delivered into the hands of men, and they shall kill him; and after that he is killed, he shall rise the third day. But they understood not that saying, and were afraid to ask him.*

And he came to Capernaum: and being in the house he asked them, What was it that ye disputed among yourselves by the way? But they held their peace: for by the way they had disputed among themselves, who should be the greatest. And he sat down, and called the twelve, and saith unto them, If any man desire to be first, the same shall be last of all, and servant of all. And he took a child, and set him in the midst of them: and when he had taken him in his arms, he said unto them, Whosoever shall receive one of such children in my name, receiveth me; and whosoever shall receive me, receivieth not me, but him that sent me.

And John answered him, saying, Master, we saw one casting out devils in thy name, and he followeth not us: and we forbad him, because he followeth not us. But Jesus said, Forbid him not: for there is no man which shall do a miracle in my name, that can lightly speak evil of me. For he that is not against us is on our part. For whosoever shall give you a cup of water to drink in my name, because ye belong to Christ, verily I say unto you, he shall not lose his reward. And whosoever shall offend one of these little ones that believe in me, it is better for him that a millstone were hanged about his neck, and he were cast into the sea. And if thy hand offend thee, cut it off: is better for thee to enter into life maimed, than having two hands to go into hell, into the fire that never shall be quenched: Where their worm dieth not, and the fire is not quenched. And if thy foot offend thee, cut it off: it is better for thee to enter halt into life, than having two feet to be cast into hell, into the fire which is never quenched. And if thine eye offend thee, pluck it out: it is better for thee to enter into the kingdom of God with one eye, than having two eyes to be cast into hell fire: where their worm dieth not, and the fire is not quenched. For every one shall be salted with fire, and every sacrifice shall be salted with salt. Salt is good: but if the salt have lost his saltness, wherewith will ye season it? Have salt in yourselves, and have peace one with another.

Here the messianic secret is explicitly stated: *This you must know, and this you must not tell anyone outside our circle! The Son of man will be killed and after three days will rise up*. Apparently Mark believes that Jesus spoke of *himself* in these words, although (once again) he speaks of a figure shrouded in mystery, "the son of man." That he speaks of himself in the third person in this way, rather than simply saying "I," casts doubt over what he said, or what he meant if he did say it. It would seem that this identity, not his words about death and resurrection, is the part that the disciples did not comprehend and "were afraid to ask him" in order to clarify. Why this fear? The idea that they were afraid to ask looks like an explanation of the disciples' tardiness to understand his true identity, something they finally came to believe in after the Resurrection-experience. Did Jesus himself so think of his identity? Again, there is no way to "go behind the text" to discover his state of mind. Probably Jesus did not think in terms of "identity" but of *vocation*: the task which God has called him to undertake, to announce the reign of God in word and deed.

Another unflattering image of the disciples follows: they are talking about which of them is the greatest and are ashamed when

Jesus catches them in such vanity. It is a very human touch in the gospel story. Jesus' word, "Whoever wishes to be first must be last of all and servant of all," is central to Christian spirituality. It is repeated in slightly different forms throughout the four Gospels. The only path to salvation—to spiritual health and wholeness—is by reversal of worldly values, dousing pride and kindling humility. Redemption demands transformation; death and resurrection is the greatest imaginable transformation. It is not complicated, but simple; it is child-like, for the path to redemption comes through the embrace of "a child like one of these."

Here follows a fast-and-furious series of sayings. First comes his response to the disciple John, who reports on their attempt to stop "a man who is driving out demons in your name" but "was not one of our following." Jesus contradicts John, concluding, "For he who is not against us is for us." In other words, one is not required to be a card-carrying member of the Jesus-movement to be accepted as working for same ends. Matthew and Luke turn the saying around 180 degrees: "Those who are not for us are against us," same thing that President George Bush said to the nations of the world after the attacks of September 11, 2001. (See Matthew 12: 30 and Luke 11: 23.) A footnote in the New Oxford Annotated Bible explains the contrary precepts as arising from different issues. But why would Matthew, who usually follows Mark closely, omit Mark's version? The more likely explanation, I think, is that Matthew, who in general is more concerned with authority in the Christian community, didn't like the open-ended implication of Mark's version of the saying, and so omitted it in favor of an alternative version, one that serves the purpose of drawing a line against outside opponents.

I call Mark's version "the liberal Jesus," one who is not jealous of his authority, not unlike "the liberal Moses"—an oxymoronic notion, to be sure. A curiously similar story tells of Joshua's complaint to Moses about men "prophesying in the [Israelites'] camp," and Moses' rebuke to Joshua: Don't forbid them! Moses declares, "Would that all the Lord's people were prophets, and that the Lord would put his spirit upon them" (See Numbers 11: 27-29.) When I cited this passage to Rabbi Marvin Bash, he said: Yes, but your "liberal Moses" was not much in evidence when he commanded the earth to open up and swallow the rebellious Korah and his men! (See Numbers 16:31.)

Indeed, my liberal Jesus quickly evaporates in Mark's Gospel, for he goes on to deliver a series of dire warnings against "anyone [who] misleads one of these little ones who have faith." But the warnings which follow, against "going amiss" by hand or foot or eye, seem more directed against personal temptations. It's not a pretty picture, and the formulaic language of these warnings allows us, I believe, to discount them.

Am I a "cafeteria reader" of the Bible, taking what I like and discounting the rest? Well, yes. Do I think we should be familiar with all of it, nevertheless, since sometimes we are surprised by insights discovered in obscure or harsh texts? Well, yes again.

The final sentences of the chapter are enigmatic and suggestive, wonderful examples of Jesus speaking "not without a parable" and leaving us to figure out what it means on our own: "For everyone will be salted with fire." Does this mean that everyone will be tested—or tasted!—as to one's spiritual quality? He continues: "Salt is good; but if the salt is salt no more [most translations say 'has lost its saltness,' as if that were conceivable], with what will you season it? Keep the salt in yourselves, and be at peace with one another." I'll make a stab at interpretation: Don't be bland, and don't be contentious, either! Follow the advice of Blaise Pascal: "Practice opposite virtues and occupy the distance between."

The only link between these fascinating verses and the scary, ascetic "I say unto thee" verses that go before is "fire." But surely "hell fire" has nothing in common with the spiritual "fire" with which we are told we must be "salted." So perhaps we can discount the warnings of hell fire for those who allow hand, foot, or eye to tempt them. Did some angry and moralistic early Christians slip in this interpretation of what "salted with fire" means? I like my interpretation better.

TWENTY-SEVEN
Whosoever shall not receive the kingdom of God as a little child

Mark 10: 1-16 *And he arose from thence, and cometh into the coasts of Judea by the farther side of Jordan: and the people resort unto him again; and, as he was wont, he taught them again.*

And the Pharisees came to him, and asked him, Is it lawful for a man to put away his wife? tempting him. And he answered and said unto them, What did Moses command you? And they said, Moses suffered to write a bill of divorcement, and to put her away. And Jesus answered and said unto them, For the hardness of your heart he wrote you this precept. But from the beginning of the creation God made them male and female. For this cause shall a man leave his father and mother, and cleave to his wife; and they twain shall be one flesh: so then they are no more twain, but one flesh. What therefore God hath joined together, let not man put asunder. And in the house his disciples asked him again of the same matter. And he saith unto them, Whosoever shall put away his wife, and marry another, committeth adultery against her. And if a woman shall put away her husband, and he be married to another, she committeth adultery.

> *And they brought young children to him, that he should touch them: and his disciples rebuked those that brought them. But when Jesus saw it, he was much displeased, and said unto them, Suffer the little children to come unto me, and forbid them not: for of such is the kingdom of God. Verily I say unto you, Whosoever shall not receive the kingdom of God as a little child, he shall not enter therein. And he took them up in his arms, and blessed them.*

On the question of divorce Jesus takes a hard line: Divorce is impossible, since "a man will leave his father and his mother, and they two [the male and the female God created] will be one flesh." So to divorce and marry another is to commit adultery, since adultery is contrary to one of the Ten Commandments delivered by Moses, specifically mentioned soon after this (Mark 10: 19). The Pharisees, however, say that the law of Moses elsewhere does allow divorce decrees to be issued by a man. Jesus says that this commandment was only issued "for your hardness of heart," in other words, as a compromise with true obedience to the law of God, allowed on account of human weakness. Jesus' judgment is hard-edged.

An interesting and insightful idea: Faith is the opposite of "hardness of heart"; it is an inclination of the heart, a heart-felt readiness to respond with kindness to the other. To be faithful is to be hardheaded and softhearted at the same time.

I note that Jesus does not object to the sexist assumption that the man holds unilateral control of the woman's fate. But his radical stance sweeps away the sexist cultural assumptions that underlie the law of divorce along with divorce itself.

I believe that divorce must be legally possible, and it can be morally right when it serves the good of both spouses and their children. (If promises never needed to be broken, we would not need promises in the first place.) Nevertheless, divorce is not an unalloyed moral good, for it involves some element of failure to fulfill one's original commitments. A marriage, a committed joining of lives and a becoming "one flesh" with another, is never utterly erased—whether or not a legal marriage has taken place. In this sense a marriage is a permanent fact, for we are changed by our relationships, and the more so, the more deeply committed our relationships. Jesus' stance reflects a radical theologizing of human existence, and leads to a surprising conclusion, namely, that *real* divorce is illusory and multiple "marriages" abound. This is offered not as advice but as food for thought!

A philosophical footnote may help, here. Historical events are permanent facts, in the sense that once they have happened they cannot be erased. Joyful events we do not want to erase, so we celebrate them annually. Sad or tragic events we might like to erase, and may try to do so, but it is a self-deception to think that we can. (And some tragedies we are morally obliged to remember.) In her profound description of "the human condition," Hannah Arendt argues that Jesus was the discoverer of "the principle of forgiveness" in human affairs. She spoke of promising and forgiving as twin necessities of moral existence: *promising*, in order to bind ourselves and others to future relationships, and *forgiving*, in order to release ourselves and others from past relationships.[48] The broken promises involved in divorce can be forgiven, but they cannot be forgotten—treated as if they never happened.

Would Jesus agree with all this, or even some of it? Or would he answer me as sharply as he answered the Pharisees? Here as always his attitude and belief are radical. He sets up a standard that *always* puts us in the wrong to some degree. It's not that he wants to humble us; it's that he makes it clear that humility is a necessity of the human condition: all of our promises and solemn covenants have been broken in one way or another, so we must forgive and ask forgiveness, so that they may be renewed. "Walk humbly with your God," the prophet Micah admonishes (Micah 6:8).

It's unfortunate that some branches of Christianity have remade Jesus' radicalism into a conservative legalism. The process of turning him into a new Moses, a law giver, began very early, as we see especially in the Gospel of Matthew. When divorce is made totally illicit, then almost inevitably, "annulment" is introduced, bringing with it the moral ambiguities of rationalization after the fact. This came to be known, pejoratively, as "Jesuitical reasoning": upholding the validity of a moral law while finding extenuating reasons for setting it aside in particular cases.

So many familiar words of Jesus are scattered through these texts! "Those whom God hath joined together, let no man put asunder." (Lattimore translates: "Then what God has joined together let man not separate.") And in the next paragraph: "Suffer the little children to come unto me, and forbid them not: for of such is the kingdom of God." (Lattimore translates: "Let the children come to me and do not prevent them; for of such is the Kingdom of God.") The language of the King James Version has found its way into our consciousness, especially through ceremonies of marriage and christening. Lattimore's and other modern translations are admirably clear, but the King James Version still casts its spell upon the imagination. It links us to a sacred tradition, and that's one of the central things that religion is all about: conveying the tradition that is held dear to the rising generation, for this goes to the core of our and their shared identity,

"Suffer the children" does not mean "put up with them," but allow them, subject your will to theirs. "Suffering" as *acceptance*, like "purity of heart" as *unreserved good will*—seem to me the opposites to "hardness of heart." For the heart, mind, and will, changeableness is a human imperative.

Our ministries are modeled after Jesus'. The minister properly holds the child for a christening or dedication: "And he embraced them and blessed them, laying his hands upon them." It is a beautiful symbolic act, a moment when parents and priest re-enact ancient sacred tradition, receiving and naming a new member of "the community of God-ruling."

TWENTY-EIGHT
One thing thou lackest

Mark 10: 17-31 *And when he was gone forth into the way, there came one running, and kneeled to him, and asked him, Good Master, what shall I do that I may inherit eternal life? And Jesus said unto him, Why callest thou me good? There is none good but one, that is, God. Thou knowest the commandments, Do not commit adultery, Do not kill, Do not bear false witness, Defraud not, Honor thy father and mother. And he answered and said unto him, Master all these have I observed from my youth. Then Jesus beholding him loved him, and said unto him, One thing thou lackest: go thy way, sell whatsoever thou hast, and give to the poor, and thou shalt have treasure in heaven: and come, take up the cross, and follow me. And he was sad at that saying, and went away grieved: for he had great possessions.*

And Jesus looked round about, and saith unto his disciples, How hardly shall they that have riches enter into the kingdom of God! And the disciples were astonished at his words. But Jesus answered again, and saith unto them, Children, how hard is it for them that trust in riches to enter into the kingdom of God! It is easier for a camel to go through the eye of a needle, than for a rich man to enter into the kingdom of God. And they were astonished out of measure, saying among themselves, Who then can be saved? And

Jesus looking upon them saith, With men it is impossible, but not with God: for with God all things are possible.

Then Peter began to say unto him, Lo, we have left all, and have followed thee. And Jesus answered and said, Verily I say unto you, There is no man that hath left house, or brethren, or sisters, or father, or mother, or wife, or children, or lands, for my sake, and the gospel's, but he shall receive an hundredfold now in this time, houses, and brethren, and sisters, and mothers, and children, and lands, with persecutions; and in the world to come eternal life. But many that are first shall be last; and the last, first.

The student lore in theological school had it that you'd get one question on the final exam in Professor Robert Slater's "world religions" course: How would a *blank*—and here he'd pick a major religion, *Buddhist, Hindu, Muslim, Zoroastrian, Jewish or Christian*—answer the question, "What must I do to be saved?" Only you wouldn't know in advance which religion he'd pick, so you'd have to bone up on all of them. Just so, the young man asks Jesus, "Good Master, what must I do to inherit eternal life?" The question is the same; a little later we hear the disciples wondering, "Who then can saved?"

It is curious that Mark, after the story of "the transfiguration" and Peter's direct avowal, "You are the Christ," tells us that Jesus deflects being called "good" since none but God alone is completely good. This is a man who claims nothing for himself and in whom others see everything they hope for, or else fear. Paradox lies at the heart of this story.

The image of the wealthy young man who, though he keeps all the basic moral commandments, cannot bear the thought of giving away his wealth for the sake of the poor, is classic. Is it that Jesus picks out the one thing this fellow most clings to? Or is he all of us, clinging to our possessions? Luke cites Jesus' beatitude, "Blessed are you poor," rather than the more familiar but spiritualized version we find in Matthew, "Blessed are the poor in spirit." It is a positive assertion of the same truth that so disappointed the rich young man: great possessions are a great spiritual impediment. The Buddha ranked this requirement even higher among those things one must do to be saved: dispossess yourself, even of your ego-centered self.

To be "saved" means to be restored to spiritual well-being, or health, as its Latin root, *salus,* and the English word, salubrious, suggest. "Eternal life" we easily equate with the idea of the immortality of the soul, a belief that Plato seeks to prove in his book, *Phaedo.* Judaism never accepted the Greek dualism of body and soul, so death must be a restoration of the whole person, body and soul, to the eternity from which the person emerged. I think of spiritual well-being in our temporal existence as the moral equivalent of eternal life, for what else is worthy of being preserved eternally, of enriching time and eternity? The Lord's Prayer says, "Thy will be done on earth as it is in heaven," praying for a duality-no-longer between the two realms, but a unity. Time is continuous with eternity; space is continuous with infinity.

Here comes the eminently quotable Jesus, again: "It is easier for a camel to pass through the eye of a needle than for a rich man to enter the kingdom of God." "For God all things are possible." "Many who are first shall be last, and many who are last shall be first." (No, he didn't say *everybody*!) Some recent interpreters speak of Jesus as a purveyor of "wisdom" sayings, like the itinerate Cynics of ancient Greece. But there is nothing wise about these statements, abstracted from the momentous events of this moment in history, this *kairos*. To turn his so-called wisdom into plain prose: (a) Great possessions tie you to worldly, self-seeking concerns. (b) Faith surrenders control, and absolute faith surrenders control absolutely; in the end, you're not in control anyway. (c) The human spirit transcends and often reverses the world's judgments, like its idea of who gets first prize.

After this section comes another famous and portentous line: "Behold, we are going up to Jerusalem." (d) Our pathways in life lead to a point of meeting, a rendezvous.

TWENTY-NINE
Behold, we go up to Jerusalem

Mark 10: 32-52 *And they were in the way of going up to Jerusalem; and Jesus went before them: and they were amazed; and as they followed, they were afraid. And he took again the twelve, and began to tell them what things should happen unto him, Saying, Behold, we go up to Jerusalem; and the Son of man shall be delivered unto the chief priests, and unto the scribes; and they shall condemn him to death, and shall kill him: and the third day he shall rise again.*

And James and John, the sons of Zebedee, come unto him, saying, Master we would that thou shouldest do for us whatsoever we shall desire. And he said unto them, What would ye that I should do for you? They said unto him, Grant unto us that we may sit, one on thy right hand, and the other on thy left hand, in thy glory. But Jesus said unto them, Ye know not what ye ask: can ye drink of the cup that I drink of? And be baptized with the baptism that I am baptized with? And they said unto him, We can. And Jesus said unto them, Ye shall indeed drink of the cup that I drink of; and with the baptism that I am baptized withal shall ye be baptized: but to sit on my right hand and on my left hand is not mine to give; but it shall be given to them for whom it is prepared. And when the ten heard it, they began to be much displeased with James and John. But Jesus called them to him, and saith unto them, Ye know that they which are accounted to rule over the Gentiles exercise lordship over them; and their great ones exercise authority upon them. But so shall it not be among you; but whosoever will be great among you, shall be your minister: and whosoever of you will be the chiefest, shall be servant of all. For even the Son of man came not to be ministered unto, but to minister, and to give his life a ransom for many.

And they came to Jericho: and as he went out of Jericho with his disciples and a great number of people, blind Bartimaeus, the son of Timaeus, sat by the highway side begging. And when he heard that it was Jesus of Nazareth, he began to cry out, and say, Jesus, thou Son of David, have mercy on me. And Jesus stood still, and commanded him to be called. And they call the blind man, saying unto him, Be of good comfort, rise; he calleth thee. And he, casting away his garment, rose, and came to Jesus. And Jesus answered and said unto him, What wilt thou that I should do unto thee? The blind man said unto him, Lord, that I might receive my sight. And Jesus said unto him, Go thy way; thy faith hath made thee whole. And immediately he received his sight, and followed Jesus in the way.

Here Jesus speaks of the central mystery that Mark means to reveal in his Gospel: "Behold we are going up to Jerusalem, and the son of man will be given over to the high priests and the scribes, and they will condemn him to death, and give him over to the Gentiles, and they will mock him and spit upon him and flog him, and kill him, and after three days he will rise." This is a précis of the Passion Story itself. Mark states his belief that Jesus is speaking of himself under the veiled title, Son of man.

This becomes the central narrative—"the story line"—of Christianity: "*We* are going up to Jerusalem." It is a mystery religion as well as a history religion, for it uses historical events as the symbolic basis of a hidden spiritual reality; to believe in it is to re-enact it. This is most easily seen in the case of the Last Supper, which is re-enacted in the ritual of Communion and participated in by the sharing of bread and wine. Just as Jesus asks the disciples whether they are really ready to "go up to Jerusalem" with him, the gospel invites and challenges us to take part in this spiritual journey.

James and John like the glory part, but the rest of it they just don't get. Jesus says, in effect: You do not know what you are asking, when you ask for seats of honor at my right and my left. His words about not granting honors, himself, but honors having been decided by God well in advance, may seem like a doctrine of predestination. It means: Under the sovereign rule of God, we all play out *the roles that we choose*, which are, at the same time, *the roles we must play*. We wonder about "the meaning of life," but it remains hidden from us until we recognize that it is something told precisely in the life we freely choose and the character we thereby display.

The story of Bartimaeus, a blind beggar sitting by the road on the way from Jericho toward Jerusalem, follows. He implores Jesus "son of David" to take pity on him; his faith, Jesus pronounces, heals him, restoring his sight; he now follows Jesus "on his way." The truth of this blind beggar's life, his character, is revealed by his faith and exemplified by his "going up to Jerusalem" with Jesus.

It is insufficiently appreciated by casual readers of the Gospels that they are not just reports of events; they are full of teaching stories. So the story of Bartimaeus teaches at least two basic things about the gospel: first, it is a spiritual reality and power that restores spiritual vision to the spiritually blind; second, it is brought by people of compassion, people who rejoice with those who rejoice and suffer with those who suffer. Does this understanding suffice for a miraculous cure? It may not be sufficient, but it is a necessary condition for activating the presence of God.

The question of miracles arises at many points for a reader of the Gospels, but what can such reports mean to us? First, we need to recognize that people in earlier ages were not basically different from ourselves. No doubt they found it easier to believe in miraculous and magical events. But for them, too, miracles were not every-day occurrences, but rare events, "wonders" almost "too good to be true." Before the scientific study of diseases, for instance, the cause of cures could be attributed to the intervention of God or other spiritual powers. From ancient times it was recognized that incantations, even by powerful spiritual healers, did not invariably produce the desired results. That is why more developed religions have given up incantation and magic in favor of prayer and faith. Prayer asks, but cannot control; faith hopes, but cannot predict. Miracles—good things happening, often beyond all reasonable expectation—depend on "the active presence of God," which I can only describe as a ready receptiveness to life and love.

Freedom is a miracle, because it's something good that happens but defies explanation. If you can explain it—tell how and why it happens—it isn't freedom.

Miracles have to do with the priority of faith over knowledge, that is, with making existential decisions about how we will relate to the world and our life in the world. Is life a good gift, and love a healing gift, or are they not? We live on a basis of *that* decision, not on the basis of scientific knowledge, nor on the basis of some pseudo-science. Thank goodness we live in an age of science, for it liberates us from superstitious religions and scientistic philosophies. Or should.

Jesus does not magically heal Bartimaeus's blindness. He says, "Go, your faith has healed you." Sounds like something God does, yet not willy-nilly, but in response to "faith." What faith? I call it a sense of the active presence of God. "Go" does not here mean "go home." Bartimaeus uses his new-found sight to follow Jesus "on his way," *going up to Jerusalem.*

Recall that when the newly exorcised "Gerasene demoniac" begs Jesus to let him go with him, Jesus tells him: No, go home and perform the proper religious rituals. A different case altogether? Ministers often have problems dealing with individuals in their churches who are neurotically dependent or disruptive, because it seems ungenerous to give them a firm "No" or, in extreme cases, a "Go away." The rule is, if he's a Bartimaeus, let him come along, and if he's a Gerasene demoniac, even a certified exorcised Gerasene demoniac, use a little "tough love" and say "No,"

THIRTY
Blessed is he that cometh in the name of the Lord

Mark 11: 1-15 *And when they came nigh to Jerusalem, unto Bethphage and Bethany, at the mount of Olives, he sendeth forth two of his disciples, and saith unto them, Go your way into the village over against you: and as soon as ye be entered into it, ye shall find a colt tied, whereon never man sat; loose him and bring him. And if any man say unto you, Why do ye this? Say ye that the Lord hath need of him; and straightway he will send him hither. And they went their way, and found the colt tied by the door without in a place where two ways met; and they loose him. And certain of them that stood there said unto them, What do ye, loosing the colt? And they said unto them even as Jesus had commanded: and they let them go. And they brought the colt to Jesus, and cast their garments on him; and he sat upon him. And many spread their garments in the way: and others cut down branches off the trees, and strawed them in the way. And they that went before, and they that followed, cried, saying, Hosanna; Blessed is he that cometh in the name of the Lord: Blessed be the kingdom of our father David, that cometh in the name of the Lord: Hosanna in the highest. And Jesus entered into Jerusalem, and into the temple: and when he had looked round about upon all things, and now the eventide was come, he went out unto Bethany with the twelve.*

> *And on the morrow, when they were come from Bethany, he was hungry; and seeing a fig tree afar off having leaves, he came, if haply he might find any thing thereon; and when he came to it, he found nothing but leaves; for the time of figs was not yet. And Jesus answered and said unto it, No man eat fruit of thee hereafter for ever. And the disciples heard it.*

We call this "the triumphal entry into Jerusalem," even though we know it will end badly. Or should I say "badly," to distinguish between the apparently bad and the really good—just as we call the day of Jesus' execution Good Friday? The depth and power of this story is intimately related to our sense of irony: what seems one thing is in truth another. No one would call Mark a sophisticated writer who would create ironic twists for literary effect. We do not imagine him composing the story he has to tell in his Gospel, but more nearly assembling it out of raw materials—probably both oral and written traditions. As previously noted, scholars speculate that he put it down on paper shortly after the destruction of Jerusalem by the Romans in 70 C. E.— an historical disaster for the Jewish people—as a way of preserving memories and records that otherwise might be lost. But more than simply "archiving" the records and memories of the nascent Christian community, Mark is weaving them into a story, so far as we know for the first time. Among canonical Biblical writings only the early letters of Paul precede Mark, and these are entirely different in character.

The entry of Jesus into Jerusalem, which Christians celebrate on Palm Sunday, seems a little anti-climatic; no sooner does he arrive than, "it being late in the day," he withdraws again, to Bethany, a village outside the ancient city. Jesus' entry into Jerusalem, riding on a colt (not an ass), is presented as a wordless symbolic act, as the earlier prophets of Israel had sometimes used symbolic acts to convey their messages. He is either deliberately acting like the Messiah, or perhaps the earliest Christians, recalling his entry and the hubbub it generated, recast it with that imagery. "Hosanna. Blessed is he who comes in the name of the Lord. Blessed is the kingdom of our father David that is coming. Hosanna in the highest!" In Jewish tradition, the Messiah, the anointed ruler of the people of God, will enter into the holy city of

Jerusalem. (Messianic expectations are reflected especially in Psalms, for instance, see Psalm 2, and in the oracles of Isaiah, for instance, see chapter 9.) Jewish tradition shapes Christian faith, and is celebrated in Christian worship ever after: "Blessed is he who comes in the name of the Lord...."

Faith is not so much concerned with historical facts, as we often suppose; it is concerned with present existence, shaped by story-borne memories and expectations.

This why worship is both sacramental, for it celebrates fulfillment, and prophetic, for it fosters hope. So Palm Sunday worship puts Jesus' coming in the present tense, as an expectation fulfilled, and in the future tense, as a hope fervently believed in.

The story of Jesus cursing an innocent fig tree, because he was hungry and it was barren, has always been difficult for morally sensitive moderns to explain. It wasn't even in season for fruiting! Rather small-minded of him, wasn't it? Or is this another symbolic action, dressed up like a literal event? Was he not only calling the Jewish establishment "barren" but even cursing it as destined to remain so "forever"? In this day of interfaith sensitivity, that's even harder to take. It is passages like this that free me from having to take a pious attitude toward everything in Scripture! There's a point at which explaining becomes "explaining away."

THIRTY-ONE

Who gave thee authority to do these things?

Mark 11: 15-33 *And they come to Jerusalem: and Jesus went into the temple, and began to cast out them that sold and bought in the temple, and overthrew the tables of the moneychangers, and the seats of them that sold doves; and would not suffer any man should carry any vessel through the temple. And he taught, saying unto them, Is it not written, My house shall be called of all nations the house of prayer? But ye have made it a den of thieves. And the scribes and chief priests heard it, and sought how they might destroy him: for they feared him, because all the people was astonished at his doctrine. And when even was come, he went out of the city.*

And in the morning, as they passed by, they saw the fig tree dried up from the roots. And Peter calling to remembrance saith unto him, Master, behold, the fig tree which thou cursedst is withered away. And Jesus answering saith unto them, Have faith in God. For verily I say unto you, That, whosoever shall say unto this mountain, Be thou removed, and be thou cast into the sea; and shall not doubt in his heart, but shall believe that those things which he saith shall come to pass; he shall have whatsoever he saith. Therefore I say unto you, What things soever ye desire, when ye pray, believe that ye receive them, and ye shall have them. And when ye stand praying, forgive, if ye have ought against any: that your Father also which is in heaven may forgive you your trespasses. But if ye do not forgive, neither will your Father which is in heaven forgive your trespasses,

And they come again to Jerusalem: and as he was walking in the temple, there come to him the chief priests, and the scribes, and the elders, and say unto him, By what authority doest thou these things? And who gave thee the authority to do these things? And Jesus answered and said unto them, I will also ask of you one question, and answer me, and I will tell you by what authority I do these things. The baptism of John, was it from heaven, or of men? Answer me. And they reasoned with themselves, saying, If we shall say, From heaven; he will say, Why then did ye not believe him? But if we shall say, Of men; they feared the people: for all men counted John, that he was a prophet indeed. And they answered and said unto Jesus, We cannot tell. And Jesus answering saith unto them, Neither do I tell you by what authority I do these things.

Perhaps, when Jesus cursed the fig tree for failing to satisfy his hunger, Mark was setting the tone for "day two" in Jerusalem, the day when Jesus enters the temple and drives out the money-changers and the sellers of doves. He was not for business as usual. He was angry and, it appears, could be violent. Had the sellers of doves and the money changers really made the Temple into a "den of robbers"? If he had put it more mildly he might have said: "You people are more intent on making a profit than on serving God, even here in God's house. Please get out." We are uncomfortable to see a Jesus who is not "meek and mild," forever turning the other cheek. We are also relieved to see him so entirely human. When the theologian Reinhold Niebuhr was asked if he thought Jesus had been "sinless," as Catholic doctrine holds, he said: Of course not: he was a man, not an angel.

Mark here sets the stage for the coming life-and-death struggle with the Temple authorities, the business-as-usual people. Their fear of him and of his popular following is noted; they are spiritually barren. As if to seal the point, Mark tells us that, on their way out of the city that evening, Peter exclaims, "Master [rabbi, in other translations], see, the fig tree which you cursed is dried up."

The answer Mark reports at this point in the story feels awkward, an insertion and a bit of a non-sequitur. First he speaks of having "faith to move mountains." This is either over-the-top hyperbole, or else it means that when you pray for something in faith you must believe that you have received it already.

The next dictum seems almost the opposite of hyperbole; it can be understood as a self-interested calculation. Jesus says that we should forgive others "*so that*" God may forgive us. This last saying is not unlike the words in the Lord's Prayer (not found in Mark): "Forgive us our trespasses as we forgive those who trespass against us." In more radical interpretation this could mean, "so that we will be forgiven," making the forgiving act causative, not merely coincidental. All this is puzzling, for it's not the usual way we think of cause and effect. Mark seems to invite this way of thinking about it. To live within the active presence of God obliterates the distinction between believing and acting, asking and receiving, forgiving and being forgiven. All these blessings are fulfilled at once. To forgive is to participate in the realm and rule of God, and this empowers the believer. It sounds like a risky way to go at life, turning heart and mind around.

So Jesus and his friends return to Jerusalem a second time, and go to the Temple. This is the second Temple, a rebuilding of Solomon's first Temple, undertaken after the Babylonian exile. Jesus is challenged by various religious authorities, "By what authority do you do this?" Rather than answer, he challenges them to answer his question: "Was the baptism [administered] of John from heaven or from men?" If they would acknowledge the God- given authority of John, then they would have to acknowledge Jesus' own authority. At least that is the implication. But, for fear of Jesus, they will not acknowledge John's authority, and for fear of "the people" they will not deny John's authority. This reflects the memory that John the Baptist's followers remained a force to be reckoned with well after his martyrdom.

Jesus' final repost, when they will say neither "yea" nor "nay" is a classic silencer. "Neither will I tell you by what authority I do these things." James Luther Adams tells another instance, pertinent to the question of Biblical interpretation. Following an address by the liberal Baptist theologian, Shailer Mathews, a man in the audience after listening intently barked out a question: "I just want to ask you, *Doctor* Mathews, do you believe that every word of Scripture is divinely inspired? Just answer me *yes* or *no!*" Mathews reflected, and then replied: "If the Spirit is greater than the letter, *yes*. If the letter is greater than the Spirit, *no*."[49] At this the Biblical literalist was silenced, for he knew what St. Paul had said: We are "competent ministers of a new covenant—not of the letter, but of the Spirit; for the letter kills, but the Spirit gives life" (2 Corinthians 3: 6). The new covenant is not a set of rules—"the letter of the law"—but a rule of love, written not in stone but in our hearts, as Jeremiah prophesied (Jer. 31: 31). The story reflects Mark's awareness that Jesus refused to make claims for himself; further, he did so *not* because it would be impolitic, or dangerous, but because it would be spiritually inauthentic, that is, an invitation to misplaced devotion. Every understanding involves at least a little leap of faith, for faith is never a secure possession. It cannot be a "letter," something you can "spell out in so many words." It is a spirit, or a way of living in the Spirit. Religious authority depends on charisma, a spiritual gift and a gift of the Spirit. To be an authority is to be an *author*, an originator, one whose works are original, seminal.

Jesus refused to be trapped into making great claims for himself. He left that to others, and seems to have succeeded beyond all reasonable expectations.

Some may ask, what makes you so sure you know what Jesus thought about all these things? I don't say I know what Jesus thought. I only know what pathways of reflection are set off in me when I read Mark's words about what Jesus said and did. Wisdom teaches that people, even those we know most intimately, remain mysterious to us; to pry without their consent, is to violate them. The German poet Ranier Maria Rilke speaks of a new kind of love, "the love which consists in this, that two solitudes protect and limit and greet each other." Less than this kind of absolute respect violates the integrity of the relationship.

Christians who affirm the divinity of Jesus know that they must at the same time affirm his humanity. Perhaps this is the reason for the mystery that surrounds the figure of Jesus in Mark's Gospel, namely, to teach an absolute respect for the humanity of the other, and in this way, also to see in each other person "the human form divine" (William Blake).

A character in a story by Andre Dubus says, "One night Father Paul and I talked about faith and all I remember is him saying: Belief is believing in God; faith is believing that God believes in you."[50] Faith, then, is an intimate relationship to the ultimate. James Luther Adams said that two things and their relationship were central to his religious and ethical thought: "the intimate" and "the ultimate." They are both intimately related and ultimately related. Religion should be studied philosophically, sociologically, psychologically, and by any other discipline, because religion and religious institutions are significant aspects of human culture. But *being religious* is always personal matter; it is part and parcel with our sense of who we intimately are and our sense of what we ultimately live for.

THIRTY-TWO
The stone which the builders rejected

Mark 12: 1-12 *And he began to speak unto them by parables. A certain man planted a vineyard, and set an hedge about it, and digged a place for the winefat, and built a tower, and let it out to husbandmen, and went into a far country. And at the season he sent to the husbandmen a servant that he might receive from the husbandmen of the fruit of the vineyard. And they caught him, and beat him, and sent him away empty. And again he sent unto them another servant; and at him they cast stones, and wounded him in the head, and sent him away shamefully handled. And again he sent another, and him they killed, and many others; beating some, and killing some. Having yet therefore one son, his well beloved, he sent him also last unto them, saying, They will reverence my son. But those husbandmen said among themselves, This is the heir; come, let us kill him, and the inheritance shall be ours. And they took him, and killed him, and cast him out of the vineyard. What shall therefore the lord of the vineyard do? He will come and destroy the husbandmen, and will give the vineyard unto others. And have ye not read this scripture; The stone which the builders rejected is become the head of the corner: This was the Lord's doing, and it is marvelous in our eyes? And they sought to lay hold on him, but feared the people; for they know that he* *had spoken the parable against them; and they left him, and went their way.*

The parable of the wicked tenants of the vineyard is an unlikely choice for "the children's hour," in church or out. It's a straightforward assertion of Jewish Christian succession to Jewish orthodoxy. ("Jewish Christian" becomes simply "Christian" when the gospel of Jesus as the Christ spreads, as it soon does, in the Gentile world.) The succession idea in the parable is clear. It asserts that the guardians of orthodoxy persecuted and stoned the prophets and finally killed the owner's son, his heir, bringing "the wrath of God"—the owner of this fruitful vineyard—down upon themselves.

Not edifying, but interesting in relation to a question that is still with us in the history of religions. The issue is the "succession" of one religion by another, and its little sibling, the appropriation—which some call "misappropriation"—of one religion's pious texts, music, and imagery by another. It may seem easy to reject "successionism"; misappropriation is not so easy to deal with, because "everybody does it."

An example follows, in Mark, of the Christian practice of "searching the scriptures" for passages in the Hebrew sacred texts that seem to prefigure the story of Jesus. The scripture cited by Jesus, "The stone that the builders rejected has come to be the head of the corner" (Psalm 118: 22-23), changes the metaphor from countryside to city—an indication that parable and narrative were married only after the fact. Both the parable and the narrative context probably reflect the destruction of the temple in Jerusalem by the Romans. If this event forms the historical background for the writing of Mark's Gospel, as many scholars believe, it seems to have decisively shaped the thought of Christians—a kind of grim proof of their case against their spiritual parents.

Thomas Whittaker, a warmly remembered teacher at Oberlin College, suggested that there are two kinds of literature, stories of father-seekers and stories of father-slayers. We were reading the Iliad and the Odyssey, texts that can be read, respectively, as father-slaying—thus "the wrath of Achilles" in defiance of king Agamemnon, and as father-seeking—thus the longing of Telemachus for his long-absent father, Odysseus. Mark, apparently, is the former, father-slaying kind—the whole authority-structure of orthodoxy being his "father." By curious twist we might say that Jesus himself is the latter, the father-seeking kind—"Abba, Father," being his God, trusted in intimate, personal relation.

The parable of the vineyard that Jesus tells draws directly on the imagery of Isaiah's poetic allegory: "Let me sing for my beloved a love song concerning his vineyard" (see Isaiah 5: 1-7), less the shocking violence in the story. Here the prophets' denunciations of the spiritual apostasies and the moral failings of God's "beloved son"—the people of Israel—becomes in Christian interpretation a foretelling of destruction, on two levels. On the literal, physical level, it foretells the destruction of Jerusalem and the Temple, and the consequent dispersion of the Jews. On the spiritual level, it foretells the cessation of Temple worship presided over by the priestly Sadducees and supported by the teaching authority of the rabbinic Pharisees. Thus Orthodox Judaism is, in Mark's view, superseded by (Jewish) Christianity.

The line between the original Jewish Christianity and the succeeding Gentile Christianity, an issue dramatized in Paul's writings, doesn't seem to have been crossed in Mark's Gospel. In other words Mark's view seems to be: "We call Jesus Messiah, the one who rules as the beloved Son of God, and so we become the true Israel, succeeding the 'establishment' Judaism which refuses to acknowledge him." It is a radical and a deeply offensive stance, portending the whole history of animosity between Christians and Jews, in spite of the fundamental dependency of Christianity on Judaism.

We feel uneasy about asserting religious "succession," since it implies superiority and has often been used to justify persecution. Religious successionism is a very old story. As Christianity with its "New and Old Testaments" claims to incorporate and succeed Judaism, so Islam claims to incorporate and succeed both Judaism and Christianity. Baha'i earns extreme antipathy from Islam by claiming to supersede the revelation given to Mohammad. Through the teachings of its founder, Bahaullah, a 19th century Persian, Baha'i claims to supersede all three faiths *by unifying them.*

The moralistic drive to purify the temple arises ever and again in the history of religion. Think of the Muslim requirement for a clean-swept place for daily prayers. Centuries ago, Hindu India horrified the invading Muslims; when I asked a wealthy Indian how he liked Singapore, he shook his head: "Too clean," he said. The anti-puritan Unitarians are in fact the genetic children of the Puritans, so-named for their zeal to purify Anglo-Catholic Christianity of its over-ripe elements. By now moralistic America is a nostalgic memory; recalling her youth in the 1950s, Sylvia Plath said, "*Pureness* is the issue."

What can we say? I love the ancient Christmas hymn, "O come, O come, Emmanuel, and ransom captive Israel." It has a solemn, Oriental flavor, and it is redolent with longing for deliverance from all that oppresses us. But is it "politically correct"? Yes, if you understand that it is not the ancient Jews but *we*, here and now, who are "captive Israel" and in need of liberation and light. The successionist idea is curiously double-edged, for it not only suggests that *we* have gone beyond *you* to a new faith, but also that *you* have laid the foundations upon which we have built. This the sense in which Christians are "honorary Jews." They receive the promise of the one God by faith, as if they were Jews by birth—at least in Christian interpretation. No wonder Christians like the idea of grace, that is, unmerited reward.

An honorific is something we do not claim for ourselves but is given to us by others. The title *Messiah* is itself such an honorific, being given to Jesus by virtue of his absolute faithfulness, although it might seem strange to call him "honorary Messiah." In the Gospels he does not ask to be appointed to this office. Rather, it is chosen for him and he remains faithful to this sacred office, "the anointed one," to the end. This understanding comports with the view of Jesus as God's son by adoption.

Note the difference, here, between the gods of Judaism and ancient paganism. We cannot imagine Yahweh as a Zeus, begetting children on mortal women! Zeus was a god who could be feared, but hardly held in loving devotion. A one sentence summary of western religious history: *Christianity grafted the Jewish God onto Greco-Roman culture.* Culturally, politically, socially, we Americans are ever so much like the ancient Romans—look at their portraits and you see, as in an antique mirror, images of ourselves, today. But a vast spiritual change happened in the late Roman empire, a time when the pagan religious system came to be seen as morally and spiritually bankrupt. What would you as an ancient Roman have felt upon hearing that Caesar Augustus, at his own insistence and on pain of death, had declared himself a god? You would have been disgusted. The Jewish God was radically different, for the cult of Yahweh had been purged of its nationalism following the Babylonian exile—in essence universalized—by the ancient prophets of Israel. The Jews instantly recognized Augustus- the-god as idolatry of the worst sort: the Absolute Power of the State. The Jews, to their everlasting credit, were the original conscientious objectors.

No wonder, then, that the early Christians had some potent talking-points, when they decided that their special mission was to bring the one God, the God of Abraham, Isaac, and Jacob, to the gentile world. They knew the difference between this unimaginable One and the god of the Absolute Power of the State. Elijah had confronted this "god" in the devotion of King Ahab and Queen Jezebel, centuries before, and his prophetic successors have done the same with respect to their despotic successors down to the present day.

The superiority of Jewish monotheism to the pagan polytheism of the time is seen in the gradual but decisive historical rejection of the latter: polytheism as aesthetic experience triumphs, as W. H. Auden notes, but serious people cannot take it seriously as a spiritual or a moral guide. The ancient gods exemplify everything vital and beautiful and grotesque; the one God is humanity's counter-player, calling our name and asking us where we are: "Moses, Moses, where are you?" Jewish monotheism is closely linked to Jewish morality, as we see in the "two tablets," the religious and the moral commands, that form the Decalogue (see Exodus 20: 1-17). In later ages Christians came to assert that the basic moral commands of Jewish law are universally applicable. The Decalogue, they said, exemplifies what the philosophers call "natural law," the law that applies to all people everywhere because it's written into our created nature.

So there is a benign side to successionism. By incorporating the past in new form, we transform and save it. Republicans were furious at President Roosevelt during the Great Depression, but historians recognize that FDR actually saved capitalism in America by transforming it into the Welfare State. Similarly, Mark and Matthew said that Jesus came not to destroy but to "fulfill" the law—saving it by transforming it.

A personal note: I have long understood my personal religious quest, within the Unitarian Universalist fold, as re-appropriation of sacred tradition. Troubled by our tendency constantly to dispossess, I have sought to re- appropriate—not to debunk but sympathetically to appreciate. This commentary is itself, as you may have sensed, a work of re-appropriation. "The stone which the builders rejected has become the head of the corner"— transformed and thereby, I pray, saved.

THIRTY-THREE
And the common people heard him gladly

Mark 12: 13-44 *And they send unto him certain of the Pharisees and of the Herodians, to catch him in his words. And when they were come, they say unto him, Master, we know that thou art true, and carest for no man: for thou regardest not the person of men, but teachest the way of God in truth: Is it lawful to give tribute to Caesar, or not? Shall we give, or shall we not give? But he, knowing their hypocrisy, said unto them, Why tempt ye me? Bring me a penny, that I may see it. And they brought it. And he saith unto him, Whose is this image and superscription? And they said unto him, Caesar's. And Jesus answering said unto them, Render to Caesar the things that are Caesar's, and to God the things that are God's. And they marveled at him.*

Then come unto him the Sadducees, which say there is no resurrection; and they asked him, saying, Master, Moses wrote unto us, If a man's brother die, and leave his wife behind him, and have no children, that his brother should take his wife, and raise up seed unto his brother. Now there were seven brethren: and the first took a wife, and dying left no seed. And the second took her, and died, neither left he any seed: and the third likewise. And the seven had her, and left no seed: last of all the woman died also. In the resurrection therefore, when they shall rise, whose wife shall she be of them? For the seven had her to wife. And Jesus answering said unto them, Do ye not there therefore err, because ye know not the scriptures, neither the power of God? For when they shall rise from the dead, they neither marry, nor are given in marriage; but are as the angels which are in heaven. And as touching the dead, that they rise: have ye not read in the book of Moses, how in the bush, God spake unto him, saying, I am the God of Abraham, and the God of Isaac, and the God of Jacob? He is not the God of the dead, but the God of the living: ye therefore do greatly err.

And one of the scribes came, and having heard them reasoning together, and perceiving that he had answered them well, asked him, What is the first commandment of all? And Jesus answered him, The first of all the commandments is, Hear, O Israel; The Lord our God is one Lord: and thou shalt love the Lord thy God with all thy heart, and with all thy soul, and with all thy mind, and with all thy strength: this is the first commandment. And the second is like, namely this, Thou shalt love thy neighbour as thyself. There is none greater commandment than these. And the scribe said unto him, Well, Master, thou hast said the truth: for there is one God; and there is none other but he: and to love him with all the heart, and with all the understanding, and with all the soul, and with all the strength, and to love his neighbour as himself, is more than all the whole burnt offerings and sacrifices. And when Jesus saw that he answered discreetly, he said unto him, Thou art not far from the kingdom of God. And no man after that durst ask him any question.

And Jesus answered and said, while the taught in the temple, How say the scribes that Christ is the Son of David? For David himself said by the Holy Ghost, The Lord said to my Lord, Sit thou on my right hand, till I make thine enemies thy footstool. David therefore himself calleth him Lord; and whence is he then his son? And the common people heard him gladly.

And he said unto them in his doctrine, Beware of the scribes, which love to go in long clothing, and love salutations in the marketplaces, and the chief seats in the synagogues, and the uppermost rooms at feasts: which devour widows' houses, and for a pretence make long prayers: these shall receive greater damnation.

And Jesus sat over against the treasury, and beheld how the people cast money into the treasury: and many that were rich cast in much. And there came a certain poor widow, and she threw in two mites, which make a farthing. And he called unto him his disciples, and saith unto them, Verily I say unto you, That this poor widow hath cast more in, than all they which have cast into the treasury: for all they did cast in of their abundance; but she of her want did cast in all that she had, even all her living.

Mark goes on to tell two stories of conflict, first with the Pharisees and the Herodians, that is, partisans of Herod the Great and his son, the tetrarch Herod Antipas. The second conflict involves the Saducees, the priestly party. The Herodians are seldom mentioned in the Gospels, perhaps because they were relatively few. Who would want to be allied with an avaricious tyrants like the Herods? They were especially interested in tax revenues, so their challenge to Jesus—after a little flattery, which he sees right through—has to do with taxes. Jesus' repost, after examining a coin with the image of Caesar, is famous: "Render unto Caesar what is Caesar's and unto God what is God's."

It has been suggested that here Jesus advocates the separation of church and state. Certainly he bases his answer on recognition that the ways of the world are not God's ways, and yet the state must be given its due. Jesus asks his interlocutors, "Why do you tempt me?" They are tempting him to speak seditious words, to justify what we call "tax resistance." He doesn't bite. But a complex nest of questions follow from this phrase, "render unto Caesar." How to protect the spiritual realm of life from the worldly realm? And how to allow the spiritual to impact, even to transform, the worldly, as every deeply spiritual soul must long for? Jesus is no hot-head, on the evidence of this story. "Cool it," he says. "Just be quite clear that what you're giving to Caesar is *not* what you're giving to God, even if it is tax deductible." The other group, the Sadducees, are oddly faceless in the Gospels. No one has even a name that would confer individuality, so they feel like set-pieces. What is being asserted here has nothing to do with particular individuals.

The second challenge to Jesus regards marriage on earth and marriage "in the resurrection," the world to come. Who will then be married to whom? Jesus' answer asserts that marriage is not something that exists among "the angels in heaven," perhaps because angels have no bodies and therefore no individuality, in traditional angelology. Marriage is a worldly matter, not a matter of eternal union. How "down to earth" of him! And yet it feels like a half-truth, for the other half of the truth is that marriage—at least if it has been what Shakespeare called "the marriage of true minds," an estate that does "not admit impediments"—is a permanent fact. If time leaves no traces in eternity, was time but an illusion? I wish we could pursue this subject with Jesus, and ask, for instance, if a man might not love all his former consorts, in this heaven of eternal, angelic forms, and they all their former lovers? But of course there is no "former" in eternity, for it must include all that has been as well as all that will be. Perhaps Jesus was a Whiteheadian well before his time.

That's one answer. The other, concluding this passage, is more radical. Responding to his questioners—"one of the scribes," a scholar of Torah— Jesus cites the book of Exodus, where the voice from a burning bush (the bush, we are told, remains "unconsumed," signifying that it is not an ordinary fire but an apparition) confronts Moses, and says, "I am the God of Abraham, the God of Isaac and the God of Jacob." (See Exodus 3: 2) Not "I *was*" but "*I am*"! Everything is present tense in this vision of the divine reality, for "God is not God of the dead but of the living." They are angels, spiritual beings who live perpetually in the presence of the one God. Thomas Aquinas said that angels have no bodies, nor histories, nor individual identities; they are outside time and history. Was Jesus a Thomist without knowing it? Another point to talk over with him.

Not only present *tense*, but present *eternally*. "The eternal present" is a phrase used by Paul Tillich to mark out the spiritual dimension of existence within which we necessarily live and to which we can potentially awaken. The dead awaken because they belong to the living promise. The pitiful and the spiteful are possessed by demonic spirits; he is possessed, over-mastered, by the Holy Spirit.

Two more short passages complete this chapter in Mark. The first is Jesus' denunciation of "scribes" who are self-important and unconcerned for the poor, but "eat up the houses of widows." No wonder "the masses heard him with pleasure," as Mark notes.

The second passage is the source of the well-worn phrase, "the widow's mite." She gives from principal (or do I mean *principle?*) while the others give only from interest (or do I mean *self-interest?*) Hard-driving church fundraisers have come up with another well-worn slogan, "Give until it hurts." New-age fundraisers go them one better: "Give until it feels good." Mega-church fundraisers never mention money, because they know it's a turn-off to Joe Sixpack, and anyway, their churches are so big that cash flow is *no pro-blem!*

THIRTY-FOUR
Take ye heed, watch and pray

Mark 13: 1-37 *And as he went out of the temple, one of his disciples saith unto him, Master, see what manner of stones and what buildings are here! And Jesus answering said unto him, Seest thou these great buildings? There shall not be left one stone upon another, that shall not be thrown down. And as he sat upon the mount of Olives over against the temple, Peter and James and John and Andrew asked him privately, Tell us, when shall these things be? And what shall be the sign when all these things shall be fulfilled? And Jesus answering them began to say, Take heed lest any man deceive you: for many shall come in my name, saying, I am Christ; and shall deceive many. And when ye shall hear of wars and rumours of wars, be ye not troubled: for such things must needs be; but the end shall not be yet. For nation shall rise against nation, and kingdom against kingdom; and there shall be earthquakes in divers places, and there shall be famines and troubles: these are the beginnings of sorrows.*

But take heed to yourselves: for they shall deliver you up to councils; and in the synagogues ye shall be beaten: and ye shall be bought before rulers and kings for my sake, for a testimony against them. And the gospel must first be published among all nations. But when they shall lead you, and deliver you up, take no thought beforehand, when ye shall speak, neither do ye premeditate: but whatsoever shall be given you in that hour, that speak ye: for it is not ye that speak, but the Holy Ghost. Now the brother shall betray the brother to death, and the father the son; and children shall rise up against their parents, and shall cause them to be put to death. And ye shall be hated of all men for my name's sake: but he that shall endure unto the end, the same shall be saved.

But when ye shall see the abomination of desolation, spoken of by Daniel the prophet, standing where it ought not, (let him that readeth understand,) then let them that be in Judea flee to the mountains: and let him that is on the housetop not go down into the house, neither enter therefore in, to take any things out of his house: and let him that is in the field not turn back again for to take up his garment, but woe to them that are with child, and to those that give suck in those days! And pray ye that your flight be not in the winter. For in those days shall be affliction, such as was not from the beginning of the creation which God created unto this time, neither shall be. And except that the Lord had shortened those days, no flesh should be saved: but for the elect's sake, whom he hath chose, he hath shortened the days. And then if any man shall say to you, Lo, there is Christ; or lo, he is there; believe him not: for false Christs and false prophets shall rise, and shall shew signs and wonders, to seduce, if it were possible, even the elect. But take ye heed: behold, I have foretold you all things.

But in those days, after the tribulations, the sun shall be darkened, and the moon shall not give her light. And the stars of heaven shall fall, and the powers that are in heaven shall be shaken. And then shall they see the Son of man coming in the clouds with great power and glory. And then shall he send his angels, and shall gather together his elect from the four winds, from the uttermost part of the earth to the uttermost part of heaven. Now learn a parable of the fig tree; When her branch is yet tender, and putteth forth leaves, ye know that summer is near: so ye in like manner, when ye shall see these things come to pass, know that it is nigh, even at the doors. Verily I say unto you, that this generation shall not pass, till all these things be done. Heaven and earth shall pass away: but my words shall not pass away.

> *But of that day and that hour knoweth no man, no, not the angels which are in heaven, neither the Son, but the Father. Take ye heed, watch and pray: for ye know not when the time is. For the Son of man is as a man taking a far journey, who left his house, and gave authority to his servants, and to every man his work, and commanded the porter to watch. Watch ye therefore: for ye know not when the master of the house cometh, at even, or at midnight, or at the cockcrowing, or in the morning: lest coming suddenly he find you sleeping. And what I say unto you I say unto all, Watch.*

Mark nicely conveys the picture of gawking by the Galilean rubes who are with Jesus in Jerusalem: "Master, what stones, what buildings!" These human touches lend a sense of authenticity to the story. Jesus dismisses their naïve wonderment and foretells an awesome wonder: it will all be destroyed. If Mark was indeed composed in the aftermath of the destruction of Jerusalem by the Romans in 70 A.D., this "prophesy" of Jesus fits perfectly. And everything that follows in this chapter, Mark's "Little Apocalypse," reflects the situation of that time for the Jewish Christians—the Jews who held that Jesus was indeed the promised Messiah.

Here are the famous warnings, in Lattimore's translation: "See to it that no one leads you astray." "Nation shall rise up against nation and kingdom against kingdom." "This is the beginning of the agony." "Whatever is given to you to say in that hour, say it, for it will not be you who speak but the Holy Spirit." "Brother will betray brother to death." "But when you see the abomination of desolation standing where it should not—and let him who reads this take note of it... ." Mark accents that his readers should take note of this prophesy, which fulfills Daniel's apocalyptic vision of the establishment of a heathen alter in the Temple of Yahweh (see Dan. 11: 31); the Roman desolation and desecration have created this vast historical crisis for the Jewish people. If we wonder, out of what white-hot passion did Christianity arise, I think we see it here: precisely out of the catastrophe of the Jewish people. From this catastrophe of 70 *anno Domini* a new faith is born, a faith in Jesus the Messiah, the anointed one of God, sent to rule on earth as in the heavens. Seventy too is a sacred number, signifying not only destruction but also fulfillment.

The first Christians did not set out to found a new religion, but to announce and endure the coming apocalypse. So even the historical catastrophe of Jerusalem is but a foretaste or a first act in the drama of the real end, the end of the world. A future, perhaps a near-future, is foreseen and this is more terrifying still. More warnings follow—it will be especially hard on women who are with child and women who are nursing "in those days." " . . . But for the sake of the chosen, whom he chose, he did cut short the days."

There follow several dire warnings against "false Christs and false prophets," reminding us that this time of catastrophe was widely felt and brought forth a myriad of responses. The by-word "be watchful" is repeated four times in this passage, including the last words of the chapter. Its effect is to heighten the sense of urgency, a mixed sense of fear and anticipation. Indeed: "Truly I tell you this generation will not pass away before all these things are done."

Mark's "Little Apocalypse" reflects the concerns of his age, a generation after the death of Jesus. The memories of the older generation, the eye- witnesses to Jesus and his brief ministry, Mark commits to writing, lest they be lost. His Gospel will be a spiritual Noah's ark. The sense of living in the End-time reflects ideas drawn from the Book of Daniel and other apocalyptic writings, for they had begun to "search the Scriptures" (see John 5:39) to make sense of the tumultuous events of the times. In a more personal way, their sense of living in an end-time may have provided psychic compensation for the catastrophic impact of Jesus' execution—seen as the beginning of the end-time.

What becomes of the kingdom of God that Jesus preached? Was he mistaken about its imminent coming? Who is to say? We make this judgment thinking that we know exactly what the kingdom God must be, but if it is a world transfigured that includes ourselves, that we stand within, we cannot know. Howard Nemerov said that a poet describes "as exactly as possible a human situation, but one that he is in." The fact that he or she is not an external observer, but is *within* the situation that is to be "exactly described" makes all the difference. To describe the humanly experienced world "exactly" means, of course, to speak truthfully. This is the deepest moral commitment that we can make, and a capability we can never once-and-for- all master. Because it cannot be done from *without* but only *within*, that is, not objectively but only existentially.

Mark says, "And then they will see the Son of man coming in the clouds with great power and glory; and then he will send out his angels and gather his chosen together… ." He means to tell us that Jesus will return as the heaven-sent "Son of man." Thus the doctrine of the Second Coming takes root in Christian belief. This returning is no distant eventuality; its power derives from its being believed as something that could happen at any moment—that's as good as present—so "be watchful" always!

And what do you or I say about this, today? When and where are we to find the long-expected kingdom of God? Here I can only speak for myself.

The image of the kingdom of God—or let us say, the community of God and occasionally, the reality of it, are to be found in the Church. "The Church" is not a particular church but the Church Universal, found wherever the dedicated community, the community of God-ruling, is coming into being. It is neither wholly past nor wholly future, but wholly present, always and only coming-into-being. And that happens everywhere, among anyone, regardless of their tradition of belief or non-belief.

That, at any rate, is the chain of thought set off in me by this astonishing fantasy, Mark's "Little Apocalypse."

The kingdom of God is present in genuine prayer, an expression of the inclination of our hearts. Simone Weil said, "Attention is an acceptable form of prayer." Being attentive is like being watchful. W. H. Auden said that faith calls upon us to take neither the past nor the future seriously, but only the present moment. Of course, he was not against either historians or science fiction writers; he knew that we are deeply influenced by the past and deeply concerned for the future. Rather, by "seriously" he meant *ultimately* seriously, a standard in relation to which all other moments, past and future, are to be judged.

THIRTY-FIVE

Take, eat; this is my body

Mark 14: 1-25 *After two days was the feast of the passover, and of unleavened bread: and the chief priests and the scribes sought how they might take him by craft, and put him to death. But they said, Not on the feast day, lest there be an uproar of the people.*

And being in Bethany in the house of Simon the leper, as he sat at meat, there came a woman having an alabaster box of ointment of spikenard very precious; and she brake the box, and poured it on his head. And there were some that had indignation within themselves, and said, Why was this waste of the ointment made? For it might have been sold for more than three hundred pence, and have been given to the poor. And they murmured against her. And Jesus said, Let her alone; why trouble ye her? She hath wrought a good work on me. For ye have the poor with you always, and whensoever ye will ye may do them good: but me ye have not always. She hath done what she could: she is come aforehand to anoint my body to the burying. Verily I say unto you, Wheresoever this gospel shall be preached throughout the whole world, this also that she hath done shall be spoken for a memorial of her.

And Judas Iscariot, one of the twelve, went unto the chief priests, to betray him unto them. And when they heard it, they were glad, and promised to give him money. And he sought how he might conveniently betray him.

And the first day of unleavened bread, when they killed the passover, his disciples said unto him, Where wilt thou that we go and prepare that thou mayest eat the passover? And he sendeth forth two of his disciples, and saith unto them, Go ye into the city, and there shall meet you a man bearing a pitcher of water: follow him. And wheresoever he shall go in, say ye to the goodman of the house, The Master saith, Where is the guestchamber, where I shall eat the passover with my disciples? And he will shew you a large upper room furnished and prepared: there make ready for us. And his disciples went forth, and came unto the city, and found as he had said unto them: and they made ready the Passover. And in the evening he cometh with the twelve. And as they sat and did eat, Jesus said, Verily I say unto you, One of you which eateth with me shall betray me. And they began to be sorrowful, and to say unto him one by one, Is it I? and another said, Is it I? And he answered and said unto them, It is one of the twelve, that dipeth with me in the dish. The Son of man indeed goeth, as it is written of him: but woe to that man by whom the Son of man is betrayed! Good were it for that man if he had never been born.

And as they did eat, Jesus took bread, and blessed, and brake it, and gave to them, and said, Take, eat: this is my body. And he took the cup, and when he had given thanks, he gave it to them: and they all drank of it. And he said unto them, This is the blood of the new testament, which is shed for many. Verily I say unto you, I will drink no more of the fruit of the vine, until that day that I drink it anew in the kingdom of God.

The Passion Story tells of the days leading up to Jesus' crucifixion in Jerusalem. We could say that the story of Passover, which underlies the Jewish feast of Unleavened Bread, prefigures the Passion of Jesus; or we could say, the Passion Story was modeled on the Passover. Christianity and Judaism, so much like Cain and Abel! The Exodus story tells that the bread at the first Passover, when the Israelites escaped from Egypt, was unleavened because they had no time to let the bread rise for baking; but this sounds suspiciously like one of those historical explanations generated long after the fact. There are many examples in the Bible—explanations that are too superficial really to explain. The true reason, I suspect, lies closer to Jesus' reason for saying "beware of the leaven of the Pharisees": leaven is yeast, and yeast is a living spirit, a mysterious and perhaps demonic power that works upon the flour, pervades the bread, and enters into those who consume the bread.

Be that as it may, Passover is a prototype of the Passion, just as Exodus is the triumphant prototype of a triumphant Easter. Both signify the dying of death and the gift of new life, called Resurrection. Some historians have questioned the identification of the Last Supper as a Passover meal; in fact, the Gospel of John does not support the identification. Mark's telling of the Passion Story is replete with scriptural "fulfillments"; with him, it's a question of meaning, not a question of plain facts. We will feel this precedence of symbolic association over fact throughout the Passion Story. How is it that Jesus seems to know what will happen at each step along the way? It is not magical omniscience; it is recognizing unfolding of events long pre-figured, and now deliberately performed. This is not fantastic; Martin Luther King, Jr. sensed his coming assassination, and alluded to it publicly several times.

James Luther Adams tells of the British newspaper that, during the end to the British occupation of India, that ran a little headline: "A New Mahatma Appears in the Ganges Valley: The Police Are After Him." Mark reports that the high priests and the scribes were after Jesus. As in India in the 1940s, they also feared provoking the populace, for Jesus was a popular hero—the kind of historical footnote that sounds like real history. This explains their turning to Judas Iscariot, as a way of capturing him quietly, without a public uproar.

The section about the anointing of Jesus by an anonymous woman seems to be interposed, as if it were a story Mark wanted to work in somewhere. The story will not sit well with the moralizers, for it rejects the moralizing of the disciples (what? waste this precious oil rather than sell it and give the proceeds to charity?) in favor of celebrating with lavish abandon. Perhaps their complaint is tinged with jealousy. (A woman? The audacity!)

A celebration, yes, but hardly a joyful one. The real significance of the anonymous woman's act is that she is anointing Jesus as both Messiah and one fated to die. Both kings and the dead are traditionally anointed with oil.

"The poor you will always have with you." Some think this fatalism, or else a right-wing slogan. But no utopian scheme has yet proved it wrong, and those who forget that the poor are with us, for all our seeming wealth, may be cushioning their consciences.

"Wherever the gospel is preached throughout all the world, what she did will also be spoken of, in memory of her." No doubt Mark would have given her name, had he known it, but he is not going to make a name up. He reports the tradition as it has come down to him, even though Jesus cannot (without omniscience) have said this as a matter of historical fact. Her anonymity does not lessen her, but exemplifies the way that this gospel story touches us. It is not a book about celebrities. She could be any of us. She will remind us of something often forgotten, that religion is fundamentally an expression of devotion: From you I receive a great gift, and to you I give my life. James Luther Adams speaks of religion as fundamentally two things, "gift and task"—we respond to the gift of life with renewed gratitude, and to the tasks to which it calls us with renewed commitment. "Devotion" seems to me to join these several moments in a seamless whole. Religious devotion is the self-giving love born of profound gratitude.

Now we go back to Judas and his quest for "an easy opportunity to betray him," as Lattimore concisely and expressively puts it. The plot thickens! And sure enough, the first part of the story of the Last Supper, which follows directly, is dominated by Jesus' warning of a betrayer among them: "One of the twelve, one who dips his hand into the dish with me... ." This meal is a most solemn celebration.

Jesus knew in advance that a man carrying a pot of water would meet them—this could be a well-laid plan, and not divine prescience—and now he knows in advance that one of the disciples will betray him. If he knows who this is, he does not let on. So there is always an uncertainty about Jesus: Does he have divine foreknowledge or simply an extraordinarily keen awareness of what is going on around him? Mark probably read it both ways, and had to do so: Absolute foreknowledge is self-contradictory, for it would make a person able to deflect future events—meaning they are no longer events in the future. I note this absurdity simply to point out that the idea that "Jesus is God incarnate so he can do anything he wants" makes nonsense of the story. It is not a fairy story but a symbol-laden history, or religiously speaking, a mystery: *a divine meaning hidden within a human story.* Christianity is a mystery religion in this precise sense: It invites participation in realities that are known only in the eyes of faith. Love—*agape*, self-giving love—is such a reality. God is another. So it's a mystery that is not exotic but in the end, commonplace, for what is hidden everywhere is hidden nowhere to those with eyes to see. Such is the mystery of the kingdom of God.

Indeed, participation in the Last Supper of Jesus with his disciples—also known as the Lord's Supper, the Eucharist, or Holy Communion—is precisely the central rite of Christian worship. The bread and the wine are elements in a mystery play, for something known only to the eyes of faith are hidden within them. Or we may better say: it is not the material elements in themselves, but the act of partaking of the bread and the wine that is the mystery, the meaning-bearing action.

James A. T. Robinson, bishop in the Church of England and noted New Testament scholar, interprets the Eucharist as "a play in four acts."[53] The "acts" are named: *taking, blessing, breaking / pouring,* and *sharing.* Note that these terms accent not the material elements but the action. Bread and wine are powerful symbols, for they can bear various levels of meaning, including body and blood; but exclusive focus on the material elements of the communion becomes macabre. When read as a dramatic narrative, the communion can be read as a story that we re-enact continually. Knowing the story's end, we can read it backwards: Partaking in this "love-feast" is *sharing* what we have broken and poured out, *breaking and pouring out* what we have blessed, *blessing* what we have taken, and finally, *taking*—setting apart—some portion of what is ours in order that we may share it with others. This circular story is a parable of *agape*, self-giving love.

There are endless levels of interpretation to these few words. "The blood of the covenant" looks back to the founding charter of Jewish and Christian faith—the bond between God and the people of God, grimly sealed in blood—and looks forward to the kingdom of God which is coming—joyous as a wedding, a love-feast. The bread is broken and shared; Jesus offers no interpretation but simply says, "Take; this is my body." Saint Paul spoke of the church as "the body of Christ," so we can say: those who together eat this bread take into themselves and become—they *incorporate*—the body of Christ. It is always taken "together," always a communal act, always a communion.

Daniel Berrigan, the Jesuit priest who devoted his life and ministry to non-violent political action, especially against war and nuclear armaments, recalled the time that a bishop rebuked him for "politicizing" the faith, saying, "The Eucharist is not political!" Berrigan replied: "Jesus didn't say of the bread, 'This is my body which is broken for me,' but 'for *you*.' If that is not a political summons, I don't know what is."[54]

Berrigan forcefully calls attention to Jesus' own act and intention, his self-giving love, an act that does not have himself but others as its object and meaning. It is symbolic action that institutes a new community centered in a sacred purpose.

These are profoundly political conceptions of faith, and belie superficial notions that the separation of church and state implies a separation of religion and politics, or of faith and action. Human action is something different from human behavior. Hannah Arendt draws the distinction with striking clarity; "behavior," she noted, belongs to "the private realm"—the household and its repetitive concerns, while "action" belongs to "the public realm"—the several forms of political community. (See *The Human Condition*, cited above.) Action is deliberate, freely decided, and potentially creative. Good actions build up bonds between people, even lasting communities.

From this understanding of "the Last Supper" as a communion which inaugurates a new community, further reflections flow. For instance: the authentic purpose of religion is not to demonstrate our own piety or virtuousness—to "save our own souls" or gain "an entrance ticket" to heaven—but to gain a greater world to live in and to live for something greater than ourselves. The title of my little book of meditations and prayers, *For Love's Sake Alone*, sought to capture the essence of that purpose. It includes these words in lines written for a chalice-lighting ritual:

> In the place of friendship there is freedom.
> Let the light we kindle go before us,
> strong in hope, wide in good will,
>   inviting the day to come.

In a footnote I credited William Shakespeare with the underlying idea: "Heaven doth with us as we with torches do, / Not light them for themselves; for if our virtues / Did not go forth of us, 'twere all alike / As if we had them not." (*Measure for Measure*, Act I, Scene 1).

In Mark, Jesus says of the bread, "Take, this is my body," and of the wine (literally, "the cup"), "This is my blood of the covenant, which is poured out for many." The phrase "for you" does not occur in Mark's account of the Last Supper, nor in Matthew's or Luke's parallel accounts (see Matt. 26: 26ff. and Luke 22: 17ff.) But in his letter to the Corinthian church (see I Cor. 11: 23- 26), Paul speaks of the communion and says that Jesus took the bread and, "when he had given thanks, he broke it, and said, 'This is my body which is for you. Do this in remembrance of me." Some ancient texts say, "*broken for you*"—possibly a late addition accenting the symbolic meanings of breaking bread with others, and of the breaking of his body. Paul goes on to say that eating this bread and drinking this cup, "you proclaim the Lord's death until he comes."

"Comes" means *comes again*, returns. Belief in "the Second Coming," not a popular belief among liberal Christians today, is rooted in the faith that Jesus' crucifixion and death were not the end, not an ignominious defeat, but a prelude to his resurrection and triumphant return—"for God will cheat no one, not even the world of its triumph." The Christian story is not one of grief and defeat but of joy and triumph—although "the time being," the time between birth and death, as W. H. Auden said, is assuredly "the most trying time of all."

More than material elements, the communion is constituted by *symbolic actions*. The bread is symbol of something that must be broken and shared, in order to be eaten. We are many bodies and together comprise one body. Similarly, the wine is symbol of something that must be poured out, in order to be drunk. We are many spirits and together share one Spirit—hot as blood, intoxicating as wine, and abundant!

The Second Coming takes on a powerful meaning when we understand it as a symbol, when "God's directive" becomes our personal and present directive in life. It becomes, then, not a story about a future event but a way of living in the "future present": living in time, consciously and affirmatively, we live toward the future, and we "invite the day to come." We cannot be what we were; we can only be what we seek. We must be transformed—all things must be transformed—on the way to fulfillment. Living between birth and death, we live by memory and hope. That is the testing and the promise of faith.

THIRTY-SIX

It is enough, the hour is come

Mark 14: 26-52 *When they had sung a hymn, they went out into the mount of Olives. And Jesus saith unto them, All ye shall be offended because of me this night: for it is written, I will smite the shepherd, and the sheep shall be scattered. But after that I am risen, I will go before you into Galilee. But Peter said unto him, Although all shall be offended, yet will not I. And Jesus saith unto him, Verily I say unto thee, That this day, even in this night, before the cock crow twice, thou shalt deny me thrice. But he spake the more vehemently, If I should die with thee, I will not deny thee in any wise. Likewise also said they all. And they came to a place which was named Gethsemane: and he saith to his disciples, Sit ye here, while I shall pray. And he taketh with him Peter and James and John, and began to be sore amazed, and to be very heavy; and saith unto them, My soul is exceeding sorrowful unto death: tarry ye here, and watch. And he went forward a little, and fell on the ground, and prayed that, if it were possible, the hour might pass from him. And he said, Abba, Father, all things are possible unto thee; take away this cup from me: nevertheless not what I will, but what thou wilt. And he goeth, and findeth them sleeping, and saith unto Peter, Simon, sleepest thou? couldest not thou watch one hour? Watch ye and pray, lest ye enter into temptation. The spirit truly is ready, but the flesh is weak. And again he went away, and prayed, and spake the same words. And when he returned,* *he found them asleep again, (for their eyes were heavy,) neither wist they what to answer him. And he cometh the third time, and saith unto them, Sleep on now, and take your rest: it is enough, the hour is come; behold, the Son of man is betrayed into the hands of sinners. Rise up, let us go; lo, he that betrayeth me is at hand.*

And immediately, while he yet spake, cometh Judas, one of the twelve, and with him a great multitude with swords and staves, from the chief priests and the scribes and the elders. And he that betrayed him had given them a token, saying, Whomsoever I shall kiss, that same is he; take him, and lead him away safely. And as soon as he was come, he goeth straightway to him, and saith, Master, master; and kissed him.

And they laid their hands on him, and took him. And one of them that stood by drew a sword, and smote a servant of the high priest, and cut off his ear. And Jesus answered and said unto him, Are ye come out, as against a thief, with swords and with staves to take me? I was daily with you in the temple teaching, and ye took me not: but the scriptures must be fulfilled. And they all forsook him, and fled. And there followed him a certain young man, having a linen cloth cast about his naked body; and the young men laid hold on him: and he left the linen cloth, and fled from them naked.

The Passion Story, as noted before, is heavily overlaid with scriptural fulfillments, an idea which treats Hebrew scripture as a prefiguring of present events. This lends the story its sense of being something that had to happen and could not have happened otherwise. Some say that this prefiguring idea makes history meaningless, for it deprives us of our freedom. But viewed from within, it makes otherwise opaque and often unbearably painful events meaningful. Thus it rescues our freedom—our inward spiritual freedom to act in ways that create and preserve meaning. Present events lose their power over us when read in the light of what has gone before. Just so, historical events in the life of Jesus were interpreted by the early Christians—Mark, almost a generation after Jesus' death, is a participant in this process—as divinely intended, and the proof of this was found in certain stories or words from the Hebrew scriptures. In this way otherwise baffling or shameful events could be understood as part of the divine intent.

We see this in the words: "And Jesus said to them: You will all be made to fail me; for it is written: I will strike the shepherd, and the sheep will be scattered; but after my resurrection I will lead the way for you into Galilee" (14: 27-28, Lattimore). The disciples remembered that they had "scattered" when Jesus was tried and crucified—probably in fear for their own lives, as well as from a sense of ignominious defeat—and this verse from the prophet Zechariah (see Zech. 3: 7) explained that unhappy fact. Jesus' direct foretelling of his resurrection and his re-appearance to them in Galilee, whence they had scattered, sounds like an explanation after the fact. If they had actually heard him say these words, they would not have been shocked and frightened by his death, but would have been confident of his and their vindication. Peter's claim that he will "never fall away" or, as Lattimore translates, will never "fail" and "disown" Jesus, emphasizes the mingled sense of defeat and shame that must have been felt among them: their spirit was willing, but their flesh was weak.

How curious that these early Christians did not cover up stories of their own ignorance, obtuseness, and weakness! They were sinners, albeit repentant sinners, and they knew it from the get-go. It colors the whole tenor of Christian faith; it is not enough to be born into the faith community, you must be "born again." Faith is never a secure possession; you must undergo conversion. The most striking expression of this idea is the story of Nicodemus, the man who comes to Jesus "by night"—that is, secretively— and asks, How can a man be born when he is old? Can he enter into his mother's womb a second time? Obviously you don't understand, Jesus says, for you must be "born of the spirit." (See the Gospel of John 3: 1-8.)

The story of Jesus with his disciples—Peter, James, and John are named— in a place called Gethsemane, is deeply affecting. "My soul is in anguish to the point of death. Stay here and keep watch," he says. Mark notes: "Going forward a little he threw himself on the ground." Albrecht Duerer's image of Jesus prostrate in Gethsemane—a masterpiece drawn in quick strokes—is profound. An angel in the clouds, beyond, holds a chalice, and there, off to one side, the disciples doze. (This image is dated 1521; an earlier etching has Jesus in Gethsemane kneeling in prayer.) Mark tells us that he prays that "this cup might pass from him"—this sacred calling, this suffering, this "cup of salvation." Salvation means spiritual healing, wholeness, fulfillment. We multiply words, but such powerful symbols as this contain many words. We are struck by the humanity of this Jesus, one who is caught in a demand that he overcome his own frailty and fear. And in this lies the double awareness of faith: that we too are called to overcome our frailty and fear in an act of final acceptance, and we are enabled to do so by casting our lot with him. He is left alone by the dozing disciples; but they were not alone, and we are not alone, even in our final hour.

Jesus' prayer in Gethsemane is what I can only call the prayer of all prayers: "Abba, father, for you all things are possible. Remove this cup from me. But *not what I wish, but what you wish*" (Lattimore translation). "*Not what I will, but what Thou wilt*" (King James Version). Sometimes prayer is denigrated as a selfish begging. But even begging need not be ignoble; it can be an acknowledgment of our human lack of self-sufficiency and need of one another. The poor call forth our compassion, and as people of faith we do not scorn the beggar at the gate, who is no more a parasite on the body politic than we.

So prayer, in the first instance, is an entirely human and indeed, a humanizing act. And *in extremis*, as Jesus' prayer bluntly reminds us, it is an act of acceptance, or perhaps we should say, "acceptance-in-faith." Death is a surrender of life. Acceptance of death is a surrender of the will to live, in trust that this final loss is part of the will of God, a will that includes the good of all people and therefore also includes me. The Lord's Prayer, which does not appear in Mark, also says it: "Thy will be done."

Jesus then finds and awakens the sleeping disciples—*Sleepers, Awake!* is one of Bach's greatest oratorios—and rebukes them for failing to wait with him, as he bade them to do. Whoever has been abandoned by friends knows the feeling; see, for instance, Jonathan Edwards's "farewell sermon" upon leaving, involuntarily, his congregation in Northampton, Massachusetts. Jesus forgives them with one of his famously useful sayings: "The spirit is willing but the flesh is weak." (Compare Richmond Lattimore's less passive translation, "the spirit is eager.") And even after this they doze off, until finally he must say, "Rise up, let us go; see, my betrayer is at hand."

The story marks a turning point: he who always acted with utter independence is henceforth to be acted upon, to suffer the will of others. *Now is the appointed hour.* This is the time of fulfillment, the *kairos*. Waiting need not be not passive; it can be a way of being in the present and, at once, of "inviting the day to come." Living in time is a mysterious thing. Is "now" only a forever-fleeting present, or something decisive, a moment to which we are fully present, fully awakened? Howard Nemerov's poem, "Moment," suggests that "the mind of God… thinks / In the instant absence of forever: *now*."[55]

In the Gethsemane story Jesus accepts his fate as one who acquiesces to the role, the calling that has been assigned to him: "the son of man." What did Jesus think of his appointment? We do not know, and Mark is oblivious to the question. The gospel, we are reminded, is a story about what God does, and where God is found, and how God finds us. It is not really written in the past tense, as a record of events long ago and far away. In the last analysis it is present tense, here and now. To have no sense of this is to be uncomprehending, to miss "the appointed hour."

Appointment is a pregnant word, meaning both a position one is assigned and the time of a meeting. Take the exmple of Abraham Lincoln: his life carries imponderable historical weight in our minds, for he was elected (that is, appointed) President and, accepting the authority of the office, he responded to the extreme demands that destiny brought to him, that is, appointed to him. We use the one word in two senses, and not only for extraordinary persons—a meeting time and place, and a designated office or role—for they are brought together in a sense of destiny.

"Betray" is another word with layers of meaning, from giving up a secret, such as revealing a hiding place and a disguised identity, to a traitorous act, such as using the privileged information of a friend to gain favor with one's enemies. All of these meanings are caught up here. "The one I kiss will be the man," Judas says, and addresses Jesus as "Master."

Some have thought that Judas's word, "Master," reflects not ambivalence or irony but rather, his being in cahoots with Jesus in the divine plan for his sacrificial death. Apparently this theory comes from some ancient Oliver Stone, for the document called the Gospel of Judas, probably dating from the second century, portrays Judas as just such a tragic hero. Alone among the disciples, he has access to Jesus' secret knowledge! This is an interesting and extreme expression of Gnostic Christianity. We can see how the seed of this thought could grow from Mark's Gospel. Equally, Mark is seminal for what became the dominant version of Christianity, as we see in the Gospel of Matthew.

Today we can be open to insights of Gnostic Christianity, gleaned from surviving manuscripts—many of which are fragmentary. The most complete of these is the collection of sayings called the Gospel of Thomas; its actual title is more precise: "The Secret Sayings of Jesus Revealed to Thomas Didymus." By comparison, orthodoxy and Gnosticism both tend toward the kind of formulaic resolutions that tough-skinned reality resists. The attractiveness of Mark is to see these issues in a form that is unresolved and invites imaginative response.

"Those who live by the sword shall perish by the sword" is another famous saying of Jesus', but Mark doesn't record it—Matthew does. The incident of one of his followers drawing his sword and striking off the ear of a slave (which Luke the physician has Jesus the good physician quickly restore!) is interesting in relation to the "resist not evil" injunction of the Sermon on the Mount (also in Matthew). The root of Jesus' non-resistance, or pacifism, can be seen in his eschatology, that is, his belief in the present, or in-breaking, kingdom of God, a realm in which the will of God totally displaces the willfulness of humans.

Only Mark notes one of the most curious events found in the Gospels—the young man dressed only in a loin cloth, who was with Jesus (the text does not say he was one of the inner circle of disciples) and loses even that covering when they try to seize him and he flees, naked. This, surely, is the raciest tidbit in all the Gospels. There are two modern speculations about this unidentified young man. Was he (as the scholar Morton Smith has argued) the homosexual partner of Jesus', there in the garden? Or was he possibly Mark himself—for how else would the writer of Mark's Gospel know about Jesus' prayer, and the other disciples being sound asleep? It is conceivable that both theories are true. As previously remarked in relation to the baptism story, the question "what eye-witness reported this story?" is probably a dead end; the story is an imaginative reconstruction of "what must have happened." Still, who could have imagined that naked young man fleeing, without an eye witness?

The quest for "the historical Jesus" generates many speculations, the truth of which are finally unknowable. Are they relevant? That depends on whether your interest is in factual history—in a realm where facts are hard to come by—or in the gospel, a story of how God entered into human history and after this, everything was changed.

Dean Samuel Miller recited for an entering class at Harvard Divinity School the words of "testy old Carlyle, in all his flamboyance." It was a cautionary tale for aspiring preachers from our reflective and gentle Dean. Said Thomas Carlyle, "That a man should stand there and speak of spiritual things to me, it is beautiful; even in its great obscurity and decadence it is among the beautifulest, most touching objects one sees on this earth. This speaking man has indeed, in these times, wandered terribly from the point; has, as it were, totally lost sight of the point, yet at bottom whom have we to compare with him? . . . Is there one worthier of the board he has? . . . Could he but find the point again!"[56]

To find the point again, consider the single sentence, "And they all left him and fled away." Jesus suffers not just death, but abandonment by his friends. We who profess to be his friends are also frail, forgetful, faulty, and desperately weak. In order to understand the gospel we must place ourselves within its story. We must read this text in the present tense, in the decisive *now*. "They" do not leave him and flee away, we do. Without this acknowledgment, we remain like Nicodemus, wondering how a grown man can enter into his mother's womb to be born again. We have wandered terribly from the point.

All things must be transformed on their way to fulfillment, even ourselves.

THIRTY-SEVEN

And Peter followed him afar off

Mark 14: 53-72 *And they led Jesus away to the high priest: and with him were assembled all the chief priests and the elders and the scribes. And Peter followed him afar off, even into the place of the high priest; and he sat with the servants, and warmed himself at the fire. And the chief priests and all the council sought for witness against Jesus to put him to death; and found none. For many bare false witness against him, but their witness agreed not together. And there arose certain, and bare false witness against him, saying, We heard him say, I will destroy this temple that is made with hands, and within three days I will build another made without hands. But neither so did their witness agree altogether. And the high priest stood up in the midst, and asked Jesus, saying, Answerest thou nothing? What is it which these witness against thee? But he held his peace, and answered nothing. Again the high priest asked him, and said unto him, Art thou the Christ, the Son of the Blessed? And Jesus said, I am: and ye shall see the Son of man sitting on the right hand of power, and coming in the clouds of heaven. Then the high priest rent his clothes, and saith, What need we any further witnesses? Ye have heard the blasphemy: what think ye? And they all condemned him to be guilty of death. And some began to spit on him, and to cover his face, and to buffet him, and to say unto him, Prophesy: and the servants did strike him with the palms of their hands.*

And as Peter was beneath in the palace, there cometh one of the maids of the high priest: and when she saw Peter warming himself, she looked upon him, and said, And thou also was with Jesus of Nazareth. But he denied, saying, I know not, neither understand I what you sayest. And he went out into the porch; and the cock crew. And a maid saw him again, and began to say to them that stood by, This is one of them. And he denied it again. And a little after, they that stood by said again to Peter, Surely you art one of them: for thou art a Galilean, and thy speech agreeth thereto. But he began to curse and to swear, saying, I know not this man of whom ye speak. And the second time the cock crew. And Peter called to mind the word that Jesus said unto him, Before the cock crow twice, thou shalt deny me thrice. And when he thought thereon, he wept.

There are two stories in this section. Curiously, here as elsewhere the second story interrupts the first. The first story tells of Jesus' trial before the Sanhedrin; Mark enumerates the high priests, the elders, and the scribes. But the second story intrudes almost from the outset: "And Peter had followed him from a distance… and was sitting there [in the courtyard] and warming himself at the fire." Was this second story, with its homey details, of greater interest? It documents the abandonment of Jesus by those closest to him, to their lasting shame.

I am reminded of what a powerful emotion shame is. We tend to discount it, as if such a low, indeed, such a *shameful* emotion, were not worthy of us. Perhaps it is not. Perhaps that's why we're so *ashamed* to admit that it could affect us. As a teenage smoker, I was shocked to see what a nasty brown stain was left in your handkerchief when you blew cigarette smoke through it! But I still didn't give up smoking until one day I was *shamed*: It seems I was playing tennis and smoking at the same time, when our esteemed leader, the Reverend Sam Wright, laughed, calling attention to the silly sight I made. Never forgot that laugh! Years later I took up something "healthier," a pipe. To cop a phrase from John Updike: Jesus, I loved that pipe! I bought tin after tin of a wonderfully aromatic tobacco blend, "Rose and Crown Tavern." It had "lotsa latakia," and people often remarked about the sweet smell. But you can't take a pipe into meetings, so I would firmly tamp down the smoldering embers and put the dormant pipe in the side pocket of my jacket. You can't waste a bowl-full of fine tobacco! The predictable happened. One day, having safely tucked my supposedly sleeping pipe into the side pocket of my nicest Harris tweed—bowl up, lest we spill any those dirty old ashes—I smelled the smell of smoldering wool. I beat it out of there to undo the damage, to my pride as much as to my beloved old jacket. Oh, the shame! The day I got smoked—that was the day I quit smoking altogether.

Don't underestimate the power of shame. Probably everyone can tell one or two good shame-stories—stories about themselves. They are hard to forget. Adam and Eve had their primal experience of shame—not the happy consciousness of being naked together but awkward self-consciousness of *being seen* naked. To be seen is to be objectified, rather than known from within. The forbidden fruit is a wonderfully ambiguous symbol, such that we'll never precisely figure it out. But we never forget once we've eaten of it, singly and together, nor are we "mortal adults" until we have done so. And by a curious turn, this awareness of being fallen also makes the experience of a second birth, a rebirth, possible. It is felt as a second childhood and a renewed innocence. The "beat poet" of the 1960s, Lawrence Ferlinghetti, rhapsodized on waiting for "a rebirth of wonder." The spiritually attuned have often spoken of a second naiveté, a consciousness found only on the far side of "paradise lost."

Let me recite a twice-told tale: "In one of her several careers, my wife, Barbara Kres Beach, was a dancing art educator. She would go barefoot in the marble halls of the Cleveland Museum of Art, leading a band of barefoot boys and girls through the paintings, responding to them in movement. The body has a language that words cannot express, and sometimes, when the language of the body is felt in the muscles and bones, movement evokes insight and gives the body voice.

"One day, Barbara was leading a group of 10 and 11-year-olds through their kinesthetic responses. First they came to El Greco's elongated, stormy- skied 'Christ on the Cross with Landscape,' and then to Murillo's exultant, cherub-strewn image of Mary, 'The Ascension of the Virgin.' 'What's a virgin, Mrs. Beach?' one child asked. Finally they came to Georges de La Tour's 'The Repentant Peter.' In the painting an aged Peter stares straight ahead, the cock that crowed stands before him. He clutches his hands together, and tears stream down his cheeks.

"Barbara had the children try out the tense gaze and the clutching gesture. 'What's happening here?' she asked. A young boy said, 'He's squeezing his hands together so tight that the water is coming out of his eyes.' When we forget, the body helps us remember.

"Barbara and the children came next to an old Dutch masterpiece, Gerhard van Hornhorst's 'Samson and Delilah.' In the painting Samson's sleeping head lies in Delilah's lap. Delilah gently takes a long lock of Samson's hair in one hand, while the other is poised for a snip. It is a moment poised for treachery. Another young boy's voice piped up: 'Finally, a Jewish picture!'

"And yet, the themes of the two paintings are not so different: a moment of betrayal, a moment portending a death. Both are images related to the primary and parallel biblical themes, Passover/Exodus and Passion/Easter."[57]

As laughter begets laughter, stories evoke stories—not diversions but illuminations.

It is interesting that Mark's story even has it that it is "one of the serving girls of the high priest," a young peasant, who puts Peter to shame—just to rub it in. His final "oath," "I do not know the man of whom you speak" is a bald lie, false to self and master! That was when the cock crowed, and Peter remembered that precisely this had been foretold; then "he threw himself down and wept." This is an example of one of the most powerful narrative devices, often called "shock of recognition."

Those who read the Passion Narrative from without, with no ear for its spiritual sense—the sense that it is self-convicting, as this story of Peter's denial so strongly shows, mistake the entire story. They construe it as an accusation directed against others, the Romans or the Jews. They think (as I once heard from a colleague in ministry) that the Gospel song, "Were you there when they crucified my Lord?" is a song of accusation, not a song of grief, sung from deep *inside* a community of faith. We are both the mindless crucifiers and the bereft friends of the Crucified.

All this encloses the very brief account of Jesus taken before the assembly of "the high priest, and all the high priests and the elders and the scribes." Mark does not use the proper term for the court, Sanhedrin, as Matthew does, either because he writes for a gentile audience or because he does not know it. "Many brought false witness against him," we are told—a direct violation of the Commandment against bearing false witness. He is innocent, Mark wants us to know.

Here we have the first direct affirmation by Jesus that he is "the Christ, the son of the Blessed One." (The Greek word, *Christos*, translates the Hebrew, *mashiah*, and the Aramaic, *meshiha*.) It is curious that Mark's Jesus, after much ado about messianic secrecy, speaks at this point not at all obliquely, but directly: "I am." Three things about this direct self-affirmation are odd: First, it seems to contradict his prior refusal to answer the question. Second, Matthew and Luke, who draw heavily on Mark, do not show him giving this answer. Third, Mark says that the witnesses against him "bore false witness," asserting his innocence, but if it was blasphemous for him to claim to be the Messiah and he did so claim, he was not innocent of that central charge. These oddities raise the question, is this a late addition to Mark's text?

In the Gospels of Matthew and Luke, Jesus turns the question back with, "You have said so," at most letting others bear witness to him. In Mark he goes on directly to assert that "you will see the Son of man sitting at the right hand of Power, and coming with the clouds of heaven," as if to say: The demonstration of what I say will come. This too is historically doubtful in this context, since the words are repeated from Mark 13: 26, where he speaks of "the Son of man" as other than himself.

I do not believe that Jesus claimed to be the Messiah or a heaven-sent "Son of man." That is a historical judgment, and one held by major New Testament scholars.[58] But far from demoting Jesus' status, this is the very basis of my understanding of his religious significance—that is, my Christology. He is "the second Adam," as St. Paul said, one who renews our humanity (1 Corinthians 15: 22). He invites us to see the essential humanity in all others, and to act in ways that affirm that recognition. We can do this, and can do it to good effect, because the realm and community of God is present all around us. This is the gospel, the good news, without which cynical pseudo-wisdom takes root in our hearts. To this proclaimed gospel only our own faith needs be added. Jesus does not claim to be the Christ, a claim that would place himself at the center and leave us arguing *ad infinitum* over whether his claim were true or false. Rather, he invites us to see the essential humanity in one another, and to love one another. He invites us to ministries of healing and teaching and organizing, not unlike his own, even sacrificing possessions and if needs be life itself for others, as he did. In a word, he invites us to be Christs to one another.

Then we can say he is the Christ to us, one who ventured far, far beyond our "comfort zone," our "weasel words," our fears and our foolish excuses. Thus poor old Peter; nevertheless he recovers his dignity to become their teacher and chief community organizer. In the Epistle to the Hebrews we read: "Since we are surrounded by so great a cloud of witnesses"—witnesses to the saving power of faith—"let us run with perseverance the race that is set before us, looking to Jesus the pioneer and perfecter of our faith…" (Hebrews 12: 1-2, Revised Standard Version). This is the gospel that Mark sets in motion, the story of a man who ventured further than any of us, blazing the way before us. I am a Gemini and often find myself of two minds; in fact (as the reader may have noticed) I like it that way. I'm with Peter, following him "afar off," at a comfortable distance. This Jesus is so frighteningly single-minded!

THIRTY-EIGHT
But Jesus answered nothing

Mark 15: 1-32 *And straightway, in the morning the chief priests held a consultation with the elders and scribes and the whole council, and bound Jesus, and carried him away, and delivered him to Pilate. And Pilate asked him, Art thou the King of the Jews? And he answering said unto him, Thou sayest it. And the chief priests accused him of many things: but he answered nothing. And Pilate asked him again, saying, Answerest thou nothing? Behold how many things they witness against thee. But Jesus yet answered nothing; so that Pilate marveled. Now at that feast he released unto them one prisoner, whomsoever they desired. And there was one named Barabbas, which lay bound with them that had made insurrection with him, who had committed murder in the insurrection. And the multitude crying aloud began to desire him to do as he had ever done unto them. But Pilate answered them, saying, Will ye that I release unto you the King of the Jews? For he knew that the chief priests had delivered him for envy. But the chief priests moved the people, that he should rather release Barabbas unto them. And Pilate answered and said again unto them, What will ye then that I shall do unto him whom ye call the King of the Jews? And they cried out again, Crucify him. Then Pilate said unto them, Why, what evil hath he done? And they cried out the more exceedingly, Crucify him.*

And so Pilate, willing to content the people, released Barabbas unto them, and delivered Jesus, when he had scourged him, to be crucified. And the soldiers led him away into the hall, called Praetorium; and they call together the whole band. And they clothed him with purple, and platted a crown of thorns, and put it about his head, and began to salute him, Hail, King of the Jews! And they smote him on the head with a reed, and did spit upon him, and bowing their knees worshipped him. And when they had mocked him, they took off the purple from him, and put his own clothes on him, and led him out to crucify him. And they compel one Simon a Cyrenian, who passed by, coming out of the country, the father of Alexander and Rufus, to bear his cross. And they bring him unto the place Golgotha, which is, being interpreted, The place of the skull. And they gave him to drink wine mingled with myrrh: but he received it not. And when they had crucified him, they parted his garments, casting lots upon them, what every man should take. And it was the third hour, and they crucified him. And the superscription of his accusation was written over, THE KING OF THE JEWS. And with him they crucify two thieves; the one on his right hand, and the other on his left. And the scripture was fulfilled, which saith, And he was numbered with the transgressors. And they that passed by railed on him, wagging their heads, and saying, Ah, thou that destroyeth the temple, and buildest it in three days, save thyself, and come down from the cross. Likewise also the chief priests mocking said among themselves with the scribes, He saved others; himself he cannot save. Let Christ the King of Israel descend now from the cross, that we may see and believe. And they that were crucified with him reviled him.

How quickly the story is told! A few brief strokes, black ink on stiff, white paper, and it is done—I think of it as a kind of calligraphy. Something terrible is happening before our eyes; the picture is not so much deliberately painted as it emerges from an unseen background. And how can we understand its meaning? To me, the story Mark is telling is neither humanly imagined nor divinely pre-ordained. Trying to understand it, we formulate antinomies: Does Jesus freely choose his fate, or is his fate imposed upon him by an inscrutable divine necessity? Mark's story is history shaped by legend and here, as always, legend is shaped by the human hunger for meaning, something worked out within the limits and the possibilities of human existence. Yes, we are free, and yet most free when we act under a moral imperative, doing what we cannot *not* do.

Meaning arises from the heart's demand that things make sense. An interpretive lens is something that helps us "make sense" of other, truly obscure things. In one sense the Passion Story recited by Mark is told in a way that reflects much that has gone before in the history of the Jewish people; in another sense, nothing like this had ever been told before. So the gospel becomes the interpretive lens of all that has gone before and all that comes after.

Matthew and Luke, but not Mark, have Jesus speak these words that interpret his fate: "Jerusalem, Jerusalem, who kill the prophets and stone those who have been sent to you, how many times have I wished to gather in your children, as a bird gathers her fledglings under her wing, and you would not let me" (Matt. 23: 37). The prophets of ancient Israel, too, were famously—notoriously!—rejected. Jesus can be called a "latter day prophet" of Israel, but he is also something so different that no traditional category or title fits. I call him the parable-teller whose life became a parable. For the Christian he is the narrow place in the hour-glass of history, the place where all that went before passes into all that comes after. What is "new" in human experience is recognized by both its *continuity with* and its *difference from* what has gone before. Such is the story before us: both deeply rooted in the past and unprecedented, radically new.

Mark assumes his readers know who Pilate is—Pontius Pilate, who had been appointed Procurator, that is, Governor, of Judea (C. E. 26-36). He is known from other contemporary histories (Josephus, Philo), and his character is similarly portrayed by them. In Mark he is compliant toward his Roman superiors; he is more interested in appeasing the crowd than in justice.

Pilate is one of the few historical anchors of the story of Jesus that finds confirmation in non-Christian historical sources. His name is even preserved in the creeds of the Church—"crucified for us under Pontius Pilate"—thus locating his story in time and place. Christian attitudes toward him vary; one tradition says he committed suicide, another (the Coptic Church) venerates him as a saint, perhaps because, like Judas, his villainy plays a necessary role in the divine drama. The lasting image, however, is of a man who "washes his hands" of responsibility, an act of weakness that betrays justice.

Jesus is charged with claiming to be "the king of the Jews," one who bears divine authority to rule the nation. Jesus neither affirms nor denies the charge that he is, or is called, "king of the Jews." That this was the charge against him seems confirmed by the statement that this title was placed over the cross of his crucifixion. Put in the mouths of his enemies, the charge that he falsely claims to be "king of the Jews" (a claim considered both seditious and blasphemous) is heard as an affirmation—unintended, yet ironically, true. The mock-royal purple vestment, crown of thorns, and the taunting words, carry out the stark irony of the theme.

Why is it that Jesus "answers nothing" to the question, "are you the king of the Jews?" Because it is neither true or false in the sense that his accusers understand. It is not true because, to a Roman like Pontius Pilate, a "king of the Jews" must be subordinate to Caesar, the emperor, and otherwise an insurrectionist. But it is also not false because he will not deny that his ministry—the transformative power of his teaching and healing—is borne by the power and presence of God.

Jesus' friends and disciples are nowhere in sight during these scenes. What witnesses could verify the accuracy of the account? Pilate himself? Barabbas, said to be an insurrectionist who had committed murder, and Simon of Cyrene, a friend, are the only other named individuals in this part of the account. We seem to be dealing with actual historical personages and events, which have become, in time, embellished by imagination. Spiritually, where in this text do we locate ourselves? The story has such depth that it can be told and retold in ways that identify us—whether reader or listener—with each of the actors within it.

This is the only answer to those who would condemn the story as anti-Semitic, in spite of the clear recognition, even preserved in later Christian creeds, that Jesus was executed as a pretender to the Jewish throne by the Roman authorities.

The meaning of the story is that we "wash our hands" of responsibility, like Pilate; we deny and betray our friends out of fear, like Peter; we fear challenges to our authority, like the priests of the Temple. Also, we fear change, like the scribes; or we join in mob actions, like the people of Jerusalem; or we have committed crimes, like Barabbas. And all of us are called upon, at one time or another, to bear the Cross, as Simon of Cyrene did—the Cross of innocent suffering for the love of others.

"Cross" is capitalized because it is not only a historical object; it is a word and an image that bears profound symbolic meaning. What it says about the limits and the possibilities of human existence is endless. But to call it a symbol is not to consider it a figment of the imagination. Mark did not make it up.

The Romans were an admirable people in many ways; they made "western civilization" possible; in their portraits, their tastes, and their literature, they appear remarkably like us. They knew many ways of dealing death, building an empire on the slaughter of millions, bringing death to whole nations. There are more efficient ways of killing criminals and enemies of the state than crucifixion, but none more well-calculated to strike terror in the hearts of the populace. It is unimaginably cruel, and exposes its victims to vast opprobrium. In a culture that celebrates raw power and worships domination—personified in the "divine" emperor—no deeper shame could be imagined than execution on a cross along with criminals. All revile the crucified Jesus—the passers-by, the high priests, the robbers who suffer the same cruel fate. The element of public shaming is notable; defeated Roman nobles were commonly offered the possibility of suicide, a private and self-inflicted death, which allowed them to preserve their dignity. By contrast we see in the shaming and prolonged torture of crucifixion a calculated act of moral degradation.

How is it, then, that Mark and the entire Gospel tradition, rather than disguise or downplay the "shamefulness" of Jesus' death, display it as a badge of honor? Rather than depict his crucifixion as unique, it is shared with common criminals. Rather than assert his power over his executioners, Jesus consents to utter subjugation to them. Rather than popular approbation, he suffers popular opprobrium. He is abandoned even by his disciples—that is, the men; a number of women "watched from afar" we are told in the passage which follows.

And yet, these very elements of the story touch us; they change our hearts. The Greek word for this kind of change is *metanoia*. These are matters that cannot be reasoned out. They turn our normal, worldly ways of understanding on their head. Rationally considered, it is nonsense, which is why Pascal famously said, "The heart hath reasons which reason knows not." The heart seeks rescue from destruction, or self-destruction, or oppression, or depression. It seeks transformation. Mark turns the Roman worship of domineering power on its head, the better to show us that the way of Jesus is the way of the transforming power of love.

THIRTY-NINE
And at the ninth hour Jesus cried with a loud voice

Mark 15: 33-47 *And when the sixth hour was come, there was darkness over the whole land until the ninth hour. And at the ninth hour Jesus cried with a loud voice, saying, Eloi, Eloi, lama sabachthani? which is, being interpreted, My God, my God, why has thou forsaken me? And some of them that stood by, when they heard it, said, Behold, he calleth Elias. And one ran and filled a sponge full of vinegar, and put it on a reed, and gave him to drink, saying, Let alone; let us see whether Elias will come to take him down. And Jesus cried with a loud voice, and gave up the ghost. And the veil of the temple was rent in twain from the top to the bottom.*

And when the centurion, which stood over against him, saw that he so cries out, and gave up the ghost, he said, Truly this man was the Son of God. There were also women looking on afar off: among whom was Mary Magdalene, and Mary the mother of James the less and of Joses, and Salome; (who also, when he was in Galilee, followed him, and ministered unto him;) and many other women which came up with him unto Jerusalem.

And now when the even was come, because it was the preparation, that is, the day before the Sabbath, Joseph of Arimathaea, and honourable counselor, which also waited for the kingdom of God, came, and went in boldly unto Pilate, and craved the body of Jesus. And Pilate marveled if he were already dead: and calling unto him the centurion, he gave the body to Joseph. And he brought fine linen, and took him down, and wrapped him in the linen, and laid him in the sepulcher which was hewn out of rock, and rolled a stone unto the door of the sepulcher. And Mary Magdalene and Mary the mother of Joses beheld where he was laid.

Jesus died, as Mark attests. "But Jesus uttered a great cry and breathed his last." We are not told that his body died but his soul was released and lived on. (The King James Version says he "gave up the ghost," which may be more poetic than "breathed his last" but is misleading if "ghost" suggests a soul or spirit inhabiting the body.) Nor is there any hint in the text that he only seemed to be dead, and re-awakened or was revived later. If Jesus really died, the Resurrection is a miracle. And not just another miracle, like turning water into wine, but the miracle of miracles. Oddly, naturalism agrees with orthodoxy: yes, he really died. But what this death means, what any death means, is not something that naturalism can tell us. It is a question of faith—a question not of "believing that" but of "believing in." The etymology of "belief" is "beloved," held dear.

Mark tells us that darkness fell over the land at the sixth hour and that Jesus died at the ninth hour. Historians say that victims of crucifixion often lasted longer than that, but it is hard to understand how such bloody torture could be endured so long. There is a deeply troubling aspect to the image of the crucified Christ, without doubt the most common religious image of Christianity in all ages. The Protestant substitution of the bare cross for the Catholic crucifix, in which the hanging body of Jesus dominates, reflects sensitivity to the gruesomeness of this dominant Christian image. In the Catholic tradition the dominantly tragic note felt in images of the Crucifixion has been softened by the contrasting sensibility reflected in the many images of the Madonna and Child. Many of the greatest Catholic churches have been named Notre Dame, for the Virgin Mary, patroness of the Church.

And yet we cannot doubt that images of the Crucifixion are among the most powerful representations of faith. To say that they "valorize violence" is to let a moralizing judgment crowd out sensitivity to deeper spiritual meanings; the same argument could be made against *Hamlet* or *The Iliad*. The greatest images of the Crucifixion evoke feelings of grief and compassion, to which the moral and spiritual ideal of self-giving love responds.

Three paintings that I have viewed in the past remain vivid in memory. Each is monumental in size, an indication of the importance vested in these works by the artists. One is the Matthias Gruenewald "Crucifixion" (1512- 1516) in Colmar, France, the central panel of a work with multiple side-panels. The figures at the foot of the cross are contorted with grief; a shockingly gruesome figure of Christ hangs before them on the cross. Another is the Diego Velázquez "Crucified Christ" (1630) in the Prado Museum, in Madrid. We see a life-size, almost naked male figure, beautifully modeled, face obscured by its downward cast, alone on the cross, against a background of a seemingly infinite darkness. The third is Peter Paul Rubens' "Descent from the Cross" (1612-1614) in the Cathedral of Our Lady, Antwerp. A baroque cascade of figures lowers the massive, deathly-white body of Jesus from the cross—an act of intense and tender piety. There's no substitute, of course, for seeing these works in person, but reproductions and commentaries are readily available on the Internet. Such images have sprung from seeds first scattered by the Gospel of Mark many centuries before.

Franz Joseph Haydn composed a cantata taking "the seven last words of Christ" as his text, the seven short sentences from the four Gospels, words said to be uttered by Jesus before he dies. Which Gospel has it right? The diversity of witnesses is happy evidence of a multiplicity of Christian understandings, and encourages us to make bold to offer our own versions, our own truths, responding to the gospel.

Mark has only one "last word" of Jesus from the Cross: "My God, my God, why have you forsaken me?" That it is given in Aramaic and then repeated in Greek would seem to testify to its being an accurate historical memory. (Aramaic is to Hebrew somewhat as Italian is to

Latin, a vernacular version.) Matthew repeats these words, with only a slightly different spelling of the words "my God." Also attesting to its historical accuracy is precisely that it seems shocking on the lips of one who elsewhere—for instance, the prayer in Gethsemane—expressed a sense of intimate communion with God, his "Abba, Father." It is curious that, here again, the Gospels retain words they might have been tempted to forget or suppress. Did Jesus really feel abandoned, not only by his friends but even by his "heavenly Father"?

The Cross signifies, at once, divine absence and divine presence. The former can be a passageway to the latter, perhaps a necessary passageway. Nicholas Berdyaev calls Jacob Boehme, a German shoemaker and philosopher in the early 17th century, "one of the greatest Christian Gnostics." (Boehme is usually called a theosophist.) He used symbols rather than concepts and invited contemplation and wisdom rather than analysis. Boehme's central insight, Berdyaev says, is "that a thing can be revealed only through another thing that resists it. Light cannot reveal itself without darkness, nor good without evil, nor the spirit without the resistance of matter."[59] God's presence cannot be known except against the background of God's absence; in fact "absence" actively resists "presence" and must be broken through by an act of will. These abstractions bring to mind the visual effect of Velázquez's "Christ on the Cross" referred to above. Once I was asked what I meant by "spirit." The question flummoxed me. Remembering Boehme's words I said: Spirit is beyond definition. In fact, it repels definition. Spirit is like the sparks that are struck from flint—something ethereal from something obdurate.

Here again the gospel invites us to contemplate a mystery: what can it mean that Jesus cries out *Eloi, Eloi, lama sabachthani*? Mark reports that some bystanders thought he was calling upon Elijah, the prophet who was expected to return as precursor to the Messiah. This indicates that some thought his words were a prayer for rescue from the cross. If so, the prayer remains unanswered, for no miraculous rescue comes. The wine mixed with myrrh, offered to Jesus before the crucifixion, was a sedative, but it is not taken. The words about casting lots for his clothing reflects Psalm 22: 18; in fact, Jesus' last words from the cross are the first line of this psalm. Some think he was reciting the words of the Psalm, and that their meaning on his lips at this time should be understood in the context of the entire Psalm. Others suggest that the Psalm was used by early Christians to embellish the crucifixion story. This is a good example of why the quest for historical certainty is a dead end. Either way, when we read Psalm 22, we see the way in which Christian piety has been shaped at its very root by Jewish piety, especially the Psalms.

Neither rational clarity nor irrational fancy, stony skepticism nor blind credulity, can account for the way that the agony of pain and abandonment transform human sensibility. Our behavior is changed; we cannot *not* be compassionate in the face of any suffering. Compassion (suffering-with) is a root-motive of morality in authentic faith traditions, notably in Buddhism and Islam, as well as in Christianity.

Is compassion rational? Paul Tillich refused to surrender the realm of the rational to emotionality or to irrationality. He spoke of "ecstatic reason" to express the experience of joyful insight, also known as a sense of breakthrough, disclosure, or revelation: "Ecstatic reason is reason grasped by ultimate concern. Reason is overpowered, invaded, shaken by ultimate concern."[60] Reason is not contradicted but fulfilled by transcending its own limitations, for it is grounded in a faith that is not itself rationally established. In his lectures Tillich commented that the word "ecstasy" comes from the Latin, *es stasis*—to stand outside oneself, as in, "I was beside myself"—with joy, or anxiety, or luminous insight. The tearing of the Temple curtain can be read as a symbol, perhaps signifying the sudden insight, opening up what had been covered in mystery: Jesus' death on the Cross, the central Christian symbol, reveals God's grace, a forgiveness available to all humanity. Perhaps this is why the first confession of faith, "In truth this man was the Son of God," comes from a Roman centurion.

Our modern minds stumble over the question, what is literally true and what is symbolic? We often say "only" or "merely" symbolic, reflecting the difficulty we have with symbolic or other imaginative forms of meaning; they may be emotionally appealing but intellectually we discount them. Such is the cracked vision of modernity decried by the visionary poet, William Blake. But we persist in asking: Is it *literally true* that "this man was the Son of God"? To say something is so "in truth" is a personal, moral affirmation, not an objective, factual observation. In Joseph Heller's suggestive phrase, "something happened," and some people told a story about it. What is literally true is that some people responded to something that happened—the life and death of Jesus—with affirmations of faith that have endured and evolved ever since.

We notice that the only witnesses to the crucifixion who are named are women, Mary Magdalene, who was exorcised by Jesus, another Mary, not here identified as the mother of Jesus, and one Salome, who Matthew identifies not by name but as "the mother of the sons of Zebedee." The first two are also named as witnesses to the place of his burial, an act of mercy carried out not by an immediate follower of Jesus by a compassionate Jew, Joseph of Arimathaea.

Against the violence of the execution stands the tenderness and reverence of the final acts of care given the body of Jesus, and the grieving mother with her adult child, famously depicted in the "Pieta" sculptures by Michelangelo, in Florence and in Rome. Musical representations are heard in the spiritual, "Were You There?" and the "Passion Chorale" of J. S. Bach, a recurrent theme in his setting of the "Saint Matthew Passion." Friedrich Nietzsche famously announced through his fictionalized Zarathustra, "God is dead, we have killed him." The statement is often cited without its latter half, which means we have killed God by forms of mental idolatry, such as trivialization and scientism. In reference to the Bach Passion music Nietzsche said, "Whoever has forgotten Christianity will hear it there again."

FORTY
He goeth before you into Galilee

Mark 16: verses 1-8 *And when the Sabbath was past, Mary Magdalene and Mary the mother of James, and Salome, had bought sweet spices, that they might come and anoint him. And very early in the morning the first day of the week, they came unto the sepulcher at the rising of the sun. And they said among themselves, Who shall roll us away the stone from the door of the sepulcher? And when they looked, they saw that the stone was rolled away: for it was very great. And entering into the sepulcher, they saw a young man sitting on the right side, clothed in a long white garment; and they were affrighted. And he saith unto them, Be not affrighted: Ye seek Jesus of Nazareth, which was crucified: he is risen; he is not here: behold the place where they laid him. But go your way, tell his disciples and Peter that he goeth before you into Galilee: there shall ye see him, as he said unto you. And they went out quickly, and fled from the sepulcher; for they trembled and were amazed: neither said they any thing to any man; for they were afraid.*

Mark 16: verses 9-20 *Now when Jesus was risen early the first day of the week, he appeared first to Mary Magdalene, out of whom he had cast seven devils. And she went and told them that had been with him, as they mourned and wept. And they,* *when they had heard that he was alive, and had been seen of her, believed not.*

After that he appeared in another form unto two of them, as they walked, and went into the country. And they went and told it unto the residue: neither believed they them.

Afterward he appeared unto the eleven as they sat at meat, and upbraided them with their unbelief and hardness of heart, because they believed not them which had seen him after he was risen. And he said unto them, Go ye into all the world, and preach the gospel to every creature. He that believeth and is baptized shall be saved; but he that believeth not shall be damned. And these signs shall follow them that believe; in my name shall they cast out devils; they shall speak with new tongues; they shall take up serpents; and if they drink any deadly thing, it shall not hurt them; they shall lay hands on the sick, and they shall recover.

So then after the Lord had spoken unto them, he was received up into heaven, and sat on the right hand of God. And they went forth, and preached every where, the Lord working with them, and confirming the work with sign following. Amen.

The oldest manuscripts of Mark's Gospel end with the 8th verse of the chapter. (The divisions of the Biblical text into chapters and verses came long after the original manuscripts were written.) If this is the original ending, it is shockingly abrupt, with nothing said about the so-called Resurrection appearances of Jesus that we have in the other Gospels. Other ancient texts of Mark continue, and there are variations in the ways they continue. Scholarly opinion holds that these verses, 9 to 20, comprise later additions to Mark's original text. The King James Version (early 17th century) and its modern successors, the Revised and the New Revised Standard versions (mid-20th century), keep this part of the text, but the modern translations carry notes calling attention to the doubtful authenticity of these verses. To end with verse 8 must always have seemed awkward and unsatisfying; the urge to fill out the story, as the other Gospels do, probably felt irresistible.

Another curious fact that any reader can easily check is that, while there is fairly close agreement among the four Gospels for the "passion narrative" (the story of Jesus' last week, ending with the empty tomb), the Resurrection narratives widely vary among the Gospels. Variation suggests later development within several independent traditions. Mark's longer ending fits this pattern.

Were verses 9-20 in Mark substituted for another, original ending, or perhaps a broken off ending? These theories have been proposed but we have no way of knowing. In addition there is another, alternative ending that is found in one ancient source, and was not included in the King James Version or in the Revised Standard Version. Lattimore includes verses 9-20, in brackets, to signal its questionable status; he also includes, in separate brackets to indicate that it is a separate ending, the following: "They reported briefly to Peter and his companions all that they [i. e., the three women who go to the tomb of Jesus and find it empty] had been told. And after that Jesus himself sent forth through them, from east to west, the holy and imperishable proclamation of everlasting salvation." This sounds like an editor's way of rounding out the story, and making its point explicit.

These are the kinds of textual questions, and perhaps confusions, that affect our understanding of the Gospels. But they should not distract us from the text itself, the words plainly before us as they have been generation after generation. What does Mark want us to know? At least this much: The male disciples having fled Jerusalem in fear of guilt by association, three women who had witnessed the crucifixion now came to the place of his tomb in order to anoint his body, an act of loving devotion. Uncertain of how they will manage the great stone that covers the mouth of the tomb, they are startled to see a young man who is "wearing a white robe."

Biblical angels usually serve as messengers from God, as this "young man" does; he is traditionally understood to be an angel. Modern interpreters often look for naturalistic explanations of Biblical stories; one such theory is that the young man was an Essene. The discovery of ancient manuscripts at the Qumran, a monastic Jewish community of Essenes in the Judean wilderness, led to speculation that Jesus had been a member of this group, spending his so-called "lost years" among them. Perhaps, then, the young man (or men) spoken of in the Gospels had come from this community to reclaim his body. This theory has led some to speculate further that Jesus was not really dead, but was released from the tomb and revived by these Essenes—providing a naturalistic explanation of the Resurrection.

Paradoxically, such naturalistic explanations tend to take Biblical texts literally, and therefore feel forced to provide literal explanations. The miracles performed by Moses—leading the Israelites through the Red Sea, providing "manna from heaven" to feed them in the wilderness, etc.—have been subjected to similar speculations. (The Red Sea could be crossed due to shallow water and a strong wind; the "manna" were migrating quail; etc.) Supernaturalism is not the only alternative to naturalism, as a way of understanding a text; often, symbolic thought can be seen to shape the way events have been remembered in a religious community. Events are given significance by being put into meaning-laden stories.

"The empty tomb" seems literal, but it is also a symbol. Luke, in his account says that the women at the empty tomb are met by two men "in radiant clothing," suggesting that they are not ordinary humans but angelic beings. Their words express the symbolic meaning of the tomb: "Why do you look for the living among the dead? He is not here; he is wakened" (Luke 24: 5-6). While not directly stated in Mark, the thought is on a trajectory from his account. The penultimate verse in Mark (the original, not the extended, text), reflects the symbolic meaning of the Resurrection in a way that is profound and moving: "He goes before you into Galilee. There you will see him, as he told you" (Mark 16: 7).

The Resurrection means: He is found among the living, among you and all living beings; and he goes before you, where you are and where all beings are. The idea that he "goes before" us is reflected in the description, previously referred to, of Jesus as "the pioneer and perfecter of our faith" (Hebrews 12: 2, Revised Standard Version), words that carry many meanings: He is one who has ventured further than we have ventured, and completed the course that we only hope we can complete. He is one who is everything that moral timidity and small-mindedness are not.

Faith is told in such metaphors, images that penetrate our life experience and place it in a context that transcends us. Karl Jaspers spoke of "the Encompassing" to denote the sense of a sacred reality that is beyond us and yet includes us. James Luther Adams spoke of "the intimate and the ultimate" as twin dimensions religious sensibility, and cited Martin Luther, "God is closer to us than our own hearts," and a sonnet by Michelangelo Buenarotti: "What leads me on… is not in me."

Mary Harrington was a colleague who, after a long interval, followed my ministry in Marblehead, Massachusetts. She gave one of the most poignant sermons I have heard, speaking while seated due to the progressive and fatal effects of ALS. She said that *when you come the point of recognizing that no one life, however long, is long enough to fulfill the hopes and dreams evoked by the precious life you have been given, then you come to terms with your innermost need, and the faith that alone can fill that need.* That precisely framed recognition became her urgent task. It is a task that we who also have "hopes and dreams" can only take upon ourselves.

> Jesus walked this lonesome valley,
>   he had to walk it by himself,
> Nobody else could walk it for him,
>   he had to walk it by himself.

The spiritual continues, "*We* must walk this lonesome valley… ."

The angel's words to the three women, "But go and tell his disciples and Peter that he is going before you to Galilee; there you will see him, as he told you," is followed by the final words in the oldest manuscripts of Mark: "And they went out and fled from the tomb; for trembling and panic had hold of them. And they said nothing to anyone, for they were afraid." This is Lattimore's translation of Mark 16: 7-8; the Revised Standard Version translates, "trembling and astonishment."

How odd that in Mark's account the angel explicitly tells them to tell Peter and the other disciples about the empty tomb, and yet "they told no one"! If so, we want to ask, how does Mark know? I imagine that he was thinking: This incident, reported only some time afterward, explains why, although his tomb *was* in fact empty, at the time nobody but these women knew about it, and at first they were too afraid to tell.

An empty tomb serves as a warning that was important to the community: Don't go looking for a gravesite with his remains! He is not there, for his resurrection was not spiritual but bodily.

The angel says that Jesus himself had told them that he would "go before you to Galilee." Mark records this in the Mount of Olives story (Mark 14: 28), in words spoken to Peter. So the angel is only repeating what Jesus had said: that after "the shepherd" had been struck down, Peter and the other disciples would abandon him; but he would rise again and appear to them in Galilee. These "predictions" reflect the memory of exactly what did happen, as the synoptic Gospels and Paul record.

In this discussion only minimal reference has been made to the other Gospels. But the stories of the resurrection appearances of Jesus in Mark can be compared to those in Matthew, Luke, and John. Close students of the Gospels readily note that the Passion Story—the last week of Jesus' life, through his crucifixion, death, and burial—is the most consistent part among them. That suggests that this was the first part of the gospel tradition to take form. But when we come to the resurrection appearances, wide divergences appear. Which suggests that these traditions were legends that arose somewhat later, among various Christian communities. They filled the religious need of the believers for themselves, for making converts, and for their children.

To me the Resurrection of Jesus is the affirmation of his person— one whose life and death gave rise to this seminal gospel story—as the embodiment of a life of self-giving love. This is as close as we can get to the divine; here the intimate and the ultimate meet. It is important, I think, to see that this is not just a story someone imagined; it is the story of a flesh and blood person, one who lived in a certain time and a certain place—just as you and I do. We either embody this way of self-giving love—wanting the happiness of the other as much as, and sometimes even more than, we want it for ourselves—or we do not. If "happiness" sounds too commonplace, use a virtual synonym, "blessedness."

A final thought, somewhat speculative though it be, on why Mark may in fact have ended his Gospel with "they said nothing to anyone, for they were afraid." This indication of an "empty tomb secret" calls to mind the idea of "the messianic secret" that runs throughout Mark's Gospel, an idea that the other Gospels soften or eliminate. It is notable that while the Gospels briefly describe subsequent "resurrection appearances" of Jesus, none ventures to describe the moment of Resurrection itself. This may simply reflect a reticence before the sacred: "Thou shalt make no graven images." For Mark (accepting the shorter text as his own), neither the foretold Resurrection nor the post-Resurrection appearances of Jesus could be described without a fundamental falsification. Belief is not a matter of evidence, even of miraculous "appearances"; belief is a gift of grace and an existential decision. Jesus' resurrection was an experience that, on the basis of testimony to his words and his deeds, his life and his death, was available to all—all who heard the story "with ears to hear."

It is available to us, today. Jesus said, "The kingdom of God is at hand." It is always at hand, always available to those who are grasped by it. When we speak of his Resurrection we do not speak of something that happened long ago, but of an interconnected chain of affirmations rooted in the gospel:

We speak, though haltingly, of *the presence of transcendence*, available to us here, now.

We grasp this presence, though imperfectly, when we exercise our *creative freedom*, the divine image in which we are made and continually re-made.

We are enabled to fulfill this freedom, though imperfectly, through *the transforming power of love, agape*.

Being graced with this sacred presence, this creative freedom, and this transforming love, we rejoice together, that we may live in concord with *the community of all souls*. Amen.

FOOTNOTES

1. "From the beginnings of the Christian way—as the gospels present them to us—the behavior that we theologians so casually call faith has shown itself as a *way* of perceiving, a *way* of acting, a *way* of holding oneself in the world of action that is God-ruling... . God-ruling is a phrase intended to underscore the dynamism and action character of *basileia tou theou*. Kingdom of God does not convey this sense of action." Richard R. Niebuhr, "Religion Within Limits," *Harvard Divinity Bulletin,* I: 2 (Winter, 1968), p. 2.
2. See John S. Kloppenborg, *Q: The Earliest Gospel* (Nashville and London: Westminster John Knox Press, 2008). For "the Gospel of Thomas," see *The Secret Sayings of Jesus,* translation and commentary by Robert S. Grant (New York: Doubleday, 1960).
3. Paul Ricoeur, "Naming God," in *Rhetorical Invention and Religious Inquiry,* edited by Walter Jost and Wendy Olmsted (New Haven: Yale University Press, 2000), p. 168. On "naming God" as a theological approach see *Naming God*, edited by Robert P. Scharlemann (New York: Paragon House, 1985), and George Kimmich Beach, *If Yes Is the Answer, What is the Question? Eight Existential Issues of Faith,* Chapter 2, "Naming God" (Madison, Virginia: Campicello Press, 2020), pp. 26ff.
4. "Christian preaching and teaching must continually re-emphasize the paradox that the man Jesus is called the Christ—a paradox which is often drowned in the liturgical and homiletic use of 'Jesus Christ' as a proper name. 'Jesus Christ' means—originally, essentially, and permanently—'Jesus who is the Christ.'" Paul

Tillich, *Systematic Theology, Vol. II, Existence and the Christ* (Chicago: University of Chicago Press, 1957), p. 98.
5. Guenther Bornkamm, *Jesus of Nazareth* (New York: Harper and Brothers, 1960), pp. 58-59.
6. Albert Schweitzer, *The Quest for the Historical Jesus: A critical study of its progress from Reimarus to Wrede* (New York: Macmillan, 1956), p. 403. The book was originally published in German in 1906.
7. Roland H. Bainton, best known for his biography of Martin Luther, *Here I Stand*, also wrote a biography of Michael Servetus, *Hunted Heretic: The Life and Death of Servetus* (Boston: Beacon Press, 1953). The historical connection between Calvinism and Unitarianism is close. Roughly speaking it is like the relationship of a father to a rebellious son; retained from the Calvinist-Puritan parent is the idea of building a holy commonwealth, or in secular terms, social reformism.
8. James Luther Adams used these "functional" terms for the personas of the Trinity in "The Ages of Liberalism," *An Examined Faith*, edited by George K. Beach (Boston: Beacon Press, 1991), pp. 337ff. Peter Fleck notes Mircea Eliade's description of an ancient tribe in which a priest impersonates the god Nishkipaz and comments: "Impersonating: the word is derived from the Latin *persona*, [which] means mask, the mask worn on the stage by the actors of antiquity.... [When the priest] put on the mask of God... he was playing God." *The Masks of Religion* (Buffalo, N.Y.: Prometheus Press, 1980), p. 6.
9. W. H. Auden, "For the Time Being: A Christmas Oratorio" (1945), in *Religious Drama: Five Plays*, ed. Marvin Halvorson (New York: Meridian Books, 1957), p. 30.
10. William Malone, "Textual Uncertainty in Luke's Account of the Baptism of Jesus," May 13, 2007, unpublished manuscript.
11. Henry Bettenson, ed., *Documents of the Christian Church* (New York: Oxford University Press, 1956), p. 37.
12. James Luther Adams, "Conversations at Collegium," *An Examined Faith, op. cit.*, p. 38.
13. George Kimmich Beach, *For Love's Sake Alone: Meditations and Prayers, The Unitarian Universalist Christian*, 50: 3-4 (Fall/Winter, 1995), p. 5.
14. On Ella Bhatt and the Self-Employed Women's Association (SEWA), see the author's blog, *www.campicello.wordpress.com*, May 19, 2011 post.
15. James Luther Adams, "Radical Laicism," *The Prophethood of All*

Believers, edited by George K. Beach (Boston: Beacon Press, 1986), p. 93.
16. James Luther Adams, "A Faith for the Free," *ibid.,* p. 52.
17. Robert Frost, "In winter in the woods alone," *In the Clearing* (New York: Holt, Rinehart and Winston, 1962), p. 101.
18. See Bart D. Ehrman, *Jesus, Interrupted: Revealing the Hidden Contradictions in the Bible (and Why We Don't Know About Them),* pp. 156ff. Ehrman cites Mark 8: 38—9: 1 and Mark 13: 24-27, 30 to support his view that Jesus was an "apocalyptic prophet," expecting the imminent end of the world, complete with an invasion by God and His angels to destroy Satan and the demons. But the scholars of The Jesus Seminar rate these passages at the lowest level of historicity; even Mark 1: 15 rates, in their color coding system, bold black type, meaning that "Jesus did not say this; it represents the perspective or content of a later or different tradition." In their view "Jesus spoke most characteristically of God's rule as close or already present but unrecognized, and thus in a way that challenged both apocalyptic and nationalistic expectations... . Like the apocalyptic view of history, the call to repentance may well have been derived from John [the Baptist]." They do not distinguish eschatology from apocalyptic fantasy, and propose that Jesus was "an enigmatic sage from Nazareth." Consistent with this view, they say, "The liberation of the non-eschatological Jesus of the aphorisms and parables from Schweitzer's eschatological Jesus is the fifth pillar of contemporary scholarship." See *The Five Gospels: The Search for the Authentic Words of Jesus,* New Translation and Commentary by Robert W. Funk, Roy W. Hoover, and the Jesus Seminar (New York: Macmillan, 1993); citations from pp. 4 and 40-41. These two views of Jesus are mutually cancelling and equally off base. I bracket the question of identifying "the historical Jesus" in favor of a close examination of our primary sources, the Gospels, to see what they reveal to us about both the origins and the outcomes of the gospel, which centrally involves but is not the same as the person of Jesus.
19. As her title indicates, a contemporary example of eschatological consciousness is found in theologian Marianne Micks book, *The Future Present: The Phenomenon of Christian Worship* (New York: Seabury Press, 1970).
20. On the concept of "parabolic vision," see George Kimmich Beach, *If Yes Is the Answer, What Is the Question? op.cit.* Chapter

8, pp. 111ff. This work was previously published as *Questions for the Religious Journey* by Skinner House Books, 1995 and 2002).
21. Frank Kermode discusses Jesus'"parable of the sower" as a key to interpreting the parables generally, in *The Genesis of Secrecy: On the Interpretation of Narrative* (Cambridge: Harvard University Press, 1979), pp. 28-29.
22. See, for instance, the commentary on Mark by B. Harvie Branscomb: "The explanation advanced in [Mark 4: 11] is an incredible one.... A parable, no matter in what form it be, is to illustrate and make clear the thought, and Jesus' parables do this to a remarkable degree." *The Gospel of Mark* (New York: Harper Brothers, 19??), p. 78. A similar but more nuanced view is held by C. M. Tuckett: " ... It is virtually impossible to see [Mark 4: 11-12] coming from Jesus himself, who (it is usually assumed) used parables to enable understanding, not to prevent it." Tuckett notes attempts "to rescue the saying for the historical Jesus—Jesus was simply reflecting on the fact that people had not accepted his message"—but remarks that "this scarcely resolves the problem of what the saying means in Mark's Greek." *Oxford Bible Commentary* (Oxford: Oxford University Press, 2000), pp. 894-895. My point is that whatever Jesus said or intended, Mark understands Jesus' utterances to have been consistently "parabolic," that is, linguistically veiled and requiring spiritual insight to be comprehended. Why? Because the kingdom of God is precisely such a spiritual reality, visible only to the eyes of faith, audible only to those "with ears to hear" (which itself is a parabolic phrase!)
23. Owen Barfield, *Saving the Appearances: A Study in Idolatry* (New York: Harcourt, Brace, 19??), p. 177.
24. Robert Frost, "Directive," *Complete Poems of Robert Frost* (New York: Holt, Reinhart and Winston, 1963), pp. 520-521.
25. Paul Ricouer, "Naming God," *op. cit.*, p. 162.
26. *The Iliad of Homer*, translated by Richmond Lattimore (Chicago: University of Chicago Press, 1951), Book 5, ll. 902-904.
27. *Augustine: Confessions and Enchiridion* (Library of Christian Classics, Vol. VII), translated and edited by Albert C. Outler (Philadelphia: Westminster Press, 1955), Book II, Chapter XXVII, p. 266ff.
28. Emily Dickinson, "This consciousness that is aware," poem 822, Johnson listing.
29. Paul Tillich, "Foreword," *Voluntary Associations: A Study of Groups in Free Societies: Essays in Honor of James Luther Adams* (Richmond:

John Knox Press, 1966), p. 6.
30. Paul Ricoeur, *op. cit.*, p. 170.
31. Kenneth Burke, "Above the Over-towering Babel," *Michigan Quarterly Review* (Winter, 1976), p. 88.
32. Vladimir Nabokov, *Speak Memory,* cited in *The New Yorker,* January 4, 1999, p. 126.
33. This simplifies a complex set of ideas by which Edwards links ontological and ethical concepts to his concept of God. See Roland Andre Delattre, *Beauty and Sensibility in the Thought of Jonathan Edwards* (New Haven: Yale University Press, 1968), p. 18ff.
34. Bethany McLean and Joe Nocera, *All the Devils Are Here: The Hidden History of the Financial Crisis* (New York: Portfolio/Penguin, 2010).
35. Alice Buchanan Lane, "The Significance of the Thirteen Women in the Gospel of Mark," *The Unitarian Universalist Christian*, Vol. 38, Nos. 3-4 (Fall/Winter, 1983), p. 18ff.
36. Soren Kierkegaard, *Fear and Trembling,* 1843.
37. See George Kimmich Beach, Chapter 6, "Newmindedness," *If Yes Is the Question, What Is the Answer? op. cit.*, pp. 82ff.
38. The idea that Jesus preached and acted upon a gospel that has profound political implications may seem surprising, even troubling. But see John Howard Yoder, *The Politics of Jesus: Vincit Agnus Noster* (Grand Rapids: Eerdmans Publishing, 1972. Yoder's "The Church As Witness to Peace" is posted on the website www.jameslutheradams.org/conversations.
39. Gerhard Ebeling, *Word and Faith* (Philadelphia: Fortress Press, 1963), p. 424.
40. "I pay a pastoral visit to a young woman in the hospital; she is seriously ill, and, after my petty complaints, I am shamed by her cheerfulness and her determination to overcome adversity. She speaks easily of herself, and I come to know her intimate fears and hopes in a way that many casual meetings would never reveal.... Is help available when I need it? It's not a comfortable question for religious liberals. We talk as if self-sufficiency were the ideal. Self-confidence, self-esteem, self- determination—the virtues of the strong and the successful—are proud words in our vocabulary. We think that we shouldn't need help... . I've been spiritually crippled by no more than a head cold! But as the young woman I saw in the hospital reminded me, I know that spiritual strength can grow when we acknowledge our weaknesses and share this awareness freely." George Kimmich Beach, *If Yes Is the Answer,*

What Is the Question? *op. cit.,* pp. 83, 87.
41. *Complete Poems of Robert Frost, op. cit., p, 27.*
42. Howard Nemerov, "The Swaying Form," cited by Douglas C. Olson in *Imagination and Spirit,* Charles Huttar, editor (Grand Rapids: Eerdmans Publishing, 1971) pp. 365ff.
43. Howard Nemerov, "Going Down in History," *The Christian Century,* November 17, 1968, quoted by permission. Nemerov's poem, "Runes," is found in his *New and Selected Poems* (Chicago: University of Chicago Press, 1960), p. 4.
44. Dorothee Solle, *Christ the Representative: An Essay in Theology after the "Death of God"* (Philadelphia: Fortress Press, 1967).
45. James Luther Adams incorporates both perspectives on the religious significance of Jesus and especially his parables for the church, "the community of communication," in his essay, "In the Beginning Is the Word," *An Examined Faith, op. cit.,* pp. *365-371.*
46. David B. Parke, "Theological Directions of Unitarian Universalism for the Next 25 Years," *The Unitarian Universalist Christian* (Fall/Winter, 1989), 44 3-4, p. 5.
47. Frank Kermode, "Hoti's Business: Why Are Narratives Obscure?" *The Genesis of Secrecy, op. cit.,* pp. 23ff.
48. Hannah Arendt, *The Human Condition* (Garden City, New York: Doubleday, 1959), pp. 212ff.
49. James Luther Adams, *An Examined Faith, op. cit.,* p. 325.
50. Andre Dubus, "A Father's Story," in *God: Stories,* edited by C. Micalel Curtis (Boston, Houghton Mifflin, 1998), p. 40.
51. Here, as so often, James Luther Adams is a ready guide to major figures in philosophy and theology. On Alfred North Whitehead, see "The Lure of Persuasion: Themes from Whitehead," on Thomas Aquinas, see "A Little Lower than the Angels," and on Paul Tillich, see "The Need for a New Language"—essays published in *The Prophethood of All Believers, op. cit.,* chapters 10, 18, and 22, respectively. Adams was a student of Whitehead and a major authority on the work of Paul Tillich.
52. W. H. Auden, "For the Time Being: A Christmas Oratorio," *Religious Drama I: Five Plays,* selected and introduced by Marvin Halverson (New York: Meridian Books, 1957), pp. 67-68.
53. James A. T. Robinson, "The Meaning of the Eucharist," in *Liturgy Coming to Life* (Philadelphia: Westminster Press, 1960). Several ideas which are woven into the book seem to form a set: the Eucharist as a series of "acts," language as "symbolic action" (Burke), sacred text as "performance" (Ricoeur), theology as

"performance of faith" (Hauerwas), kingdom of God as "God-ruling" (R. R. Niebuhr), metaphysics as "process" (Whitehead) or "method" (Lonergan), thinking as "the dialogue of the mind with itself" (Plato), gospel as "speaking in parables" (Jesus of Nazareth).

54. Fr. Daniel Berrigan said this at a conference of the Collegium Association of Liberal Religious Scholars, in October, 2007, at Craigville, Massachusetts. He had come at the invitation of my colleague in ministry, the late Rev. Paul Sawyer.
55. Howard Nemerov, lines from "Moment," *New and Selected Poems* Chicago: University of Chicago Press, 1960), p. 3.
56. Samuel H. Miller, "But to Find the Point Again," *Contemporary Accents in Liberal Religion*, Bradford E. Gale, editor (Boston: Beacon Press, 1960), p. 78.
57. George Kimmich Beach, *If Yes Is the Answer, What Is the Question? op. cit.*, pp. 106-107.
58. See, for instance, the discussion of this question by Guenther Bornkamm, *Jesus of Nazareth, op. cit.*, pp. 169ff.
59. Nicholas Berdyaev, "Introduction" to *Six Theosophic Points*, by Jakob Boehme (Ann Arbor: University of Michigan Press, 1958), p. xi.
60. Paul Tillich, *Systematic Theology* (Chicago: University of Chicago Press, 1951), Vol. I, p. 52.

www.ingramcontent.com/pod-product-compliance
Lightning Source LLC
LaVergne TN
LVHW091536060526
838200LV00036B/629